the

Paris

wedding

the *Paris* wedding

KIMBERLEY PETYT

**GIBBS SMITH**
TO ENRICH AND INSPIRE HUMANKIND

First Edition
17 16 15 14 13      5 4 3 2 1

Published by
Gibbs Smith
P.O. Box 667
Layton, Utah 84041

1.800.835.4993 orders
www.gibbs-smith.com

Designed by Sheryl Dickert
Printed and bound in China

Gibbs Smith books are printed on either recycled, 100% post-consumer waste, FSC-certified papers or on paper produced from sustainable PEFC-certified forest/controlled wood source. Learn more at www.pefc.org.

Library of Congress Cataloging-in-Publication Data

Petyt, Kimberley.
  The Paris wedding / Kimberley Petyt. — First Edition.
    pages cm
  ISBN 978-1-4236-3065-4
1. Destination weddings—France—Paris. I. Title.
  HQ745.P46 2013
  392.50944'361—dc23
                2012033146

*To Auntie Carol, mom, dad, Lamar, my babies and*
*mon amour—for your love and support.*

# Contents

# Acknowledgments

So many people helped to make this book possible. I want to thank Laurie Pike and Astrid Mueller for setting the wheels in motion. My agent, Deborah Ritchkin, and editor, Hollie Keith, for making it actually happen. My entire family for their constant, unwavering encouragement. "My People" for always loving and supporting me: Tamiko, Paula, Joli, Amy, Bruce, Tracy and the rest of the gang. My Paris posse: Photographer Ian Holmes, guardian angels Kim Poulin and Rhys Jervis, Mina and Alain from Atelier Lieu-Dit, Les Familles Petyt, Verove et Talleu (for their support AND for letting me forage through their basements and attics), the girls (past and present) from Sugarplum Cake Shop, Sarah Livescault from Mister M Studio, Mark Williamson from Maceo Restaurant, Keiran Gleeson from Global Style Management, Frédéric from Dany Art Deco & BDV Decoration, Heidi and Jason from Au Grenier de Lucie, Photographer Jo-Zhou Xiaonan, Christy Toney from CT Designs Wedding & Calligraphy (honorary Parisian!) and Christina Halstead for the use of her beautiful home. Thank you to all of the photographers and clients who allowed me to share their images in this book. Most of all—thanks to my babies for surviving a year of stress-bomb mama, and to *mon amour*—without whom none of this would've been possible. Literally.

# Introduction

From the classic Technicolor dance scenes of *An American in Paris* to more recent films like *Amelie Poulain* and *Midnight in Paris,* for many Americans, Paris is the epitome of style and romance. And what could be a more romantic place to get married? After deciding to get married in Paris, the first thing most couples do is make a giddy, "so crazy this just might work" phone call to their local French consulate where they are instantly brought back down to Earth by their first encounter with the infamous French bureaucracy: *"Quoi?! Non! Les étrangers ne peuvent JAMAIS avoir un mariage civil en France s'ils ne vivent pas en France. Impossible! Au revoir!"* ("What?! No! Foreigners may NEVER have a French civil wedding if they do not live in France. Impossible! Good-bye!") Click . . . And for some couples, that will be that. In a flash, they've swept directly to Plan B, their local country club with an impersonal, pre-packaged "One Night in Paris" themed reception. Do not pass *"Départ."* Do not collect 200€.

My own wedding adventure wasn't quite as perilous. My husband is French, and with his mother and sister in the trenches for us, we were able to plan our wedding in France long distance from San Francisco. That's not to say planning a wedding in a foreign country 3,000 miles away was a cakewalk. One main roadblock was that I didn't speak French, and my husband's family didn't speak English, which made my sole method of communication with my in-laws via my French-born, "weddingly challenged" husband-to-be. I remember standing behind him in silent anguish during one of his family phone calls as I listened to him try to translate the color sage to his sister. *Le pauvre* (poor guy), it's a wonder he went through with the wedding at all.

Besides the language barriers, the cultural aspects of the American Wedding Machine played a big part in my wedding frustrations. For example, back when we got married, no self-respecting Follower of Martha would dare to NOT offer her guests a favor trussed up in a mini Chinese takeout box. In the midst of my destination-wedding-planning frenzy, I had to rely on my husband to explain to his *maman* in a tiny town in the North of France:

What Chinese takeout was . . .

What Chinese takeout boxes were . . .

What an American wedding favor was . . .

. . . and why his American wife didn't want traditional French chocolate-almond dragées for her wedding favors (when what I really didn't want were the pastel tulle and satin ribbon sachets they came in).

Language, legal and cultural roadblocks aside, in the end our wedding was perfect—with just the right mix of French and American traditions to make both of our mamans happy.

Soon after our wedding, we moved to Paris and started our family. Within a few years, I began to plot out the next phase of my life. Remembering my "colorful" wedding-planning adventure, I realized that there must be other hopelessly romantic, monolingual Francophiles just dying to get married in Paris. So, tapping into my corporate and social event-planning background, I decided to create a wedding-planning agency, "Parisian Events—for stylish Parisian celebrations" in 2006. I started blogging about my adventures in 2007.

Since the beginning, my wedding clients have primarily been either dual-Anglophone (couples who both have come to Paris from English-speaking countries specifically for their celebration) or locally based Franco-American (usually American brides in Paris who are marrying French husbands). Because of this, the raison d'être behind Parisian Events has always been to creatively blend traditional American elements (like coordinated bridesmaids, multilayered stacked cakes or funky and original wedding favors) with classic Parisian elegance to create unforgettable, once-in-a-lifetime celebrations.

While it doesn't have to cost an arm and a leg, I know that it's not in everyone's budget to be able to host a wedding or special event in Paris. Francophiles around the world would agree that what sets French weddings apart is their inherent refined elegance. Fortunately, with a little know-how, this elegance is something that can be brought to French-*inspired* celebrations anywhere—and for nearly any budget. That's why I've written this book, as an ideas-packed, go-to guide for globally minded trendsetters who are, above all else, in love with the style, romance and refined elegance of Paris, whether they have the means to physically make the trip or not.

In addition to being a resource of practical information for those planning a wedding IN Paris (legal requirements for marrying in Paris, how to get married in a church in France, what to wear to a French wedding, etc.), I've also opened up my personal Black Book to help you to define your Parisian wedding style: I share stylish tips and insider info on choosing top-of-the-line professionals and resources, both in Paris and around the globe, to help you add that Parisian *je ne sais quoi* (certain something) to your *fête fabuleux* (fabulous party)—no matter where you're hosting your celebration.

# The Skinny on Getting Married in Paris

WHAT COULD BE MORE STYLISH AND ROMANTIC THAN A WEDDING IN PARIS? WITH THE RISE IN POPULARITY OF DESTINATION WEDDINGS AND THE THRIVING HOSPITALITY INDUSTRY THAT CATERS TO THEM, PARIS HAS BECOME AS VIABLE A DESTINATION OPTION TO THE NEWLY ENGAGED AS A WEDDING ON EITHER COAST OF THE UNITED STATES. UNFORTUNATELY, ALONGSIDE THE FAIRYTALE IMAGES OF A PARISIAN WEDDING IS THE HARSH REALITY OF MILES AND MILES OF ADMINISTRATIVE RED TAPE.

One of the biggest obstacles for you love-struck couples who want to get married in Paris is that in order to be legally wed in France, at least one of you needs to have lived in France, in the district around the city hall in which you plan to get married, for a minimum of forty consecutive days before the wedding. This includes the additional ten days for the city hall to publish the *banns*—a public announcement that is put up in the city hall for ten days before your marriage that lists your names and your wedding date so that any estranged husbands or wives have one last chance to find you before you're married off.

Before asking for that sabbatical from work, though, you should know that this one little detail is actually a pretty big one. In order to prove residency, you'll need to show two separate official documents that show your French address (called a *justificatif de domicile*) such as a gas or electricity bill, a rent receipt, a French social security insurance card or a car leasing agreement. And just in case you've got the bright idea to rent an apartment in Paris on a short-term lease in order to meet this legal requirement, you need to know that it could take several months before you receive some of those documents.

If you're not able to rent your own apartment, another option is for you and/or your honey to move in with a friend or relative in your desired district, and have that person sign an attestation *d'hébergement sur l'honneur*. This is a statement swearing that you have been living in that person's home, and that they take full responsibility for you if you happen to be an illegal truffle trafficker or something. There is a ton of small print attached to this document, including a huge fine and a short trip to the guillotine if it's ever found out that you were not, in fact, living with them. Know that this is a pretty big favor that you'd be asking of someone.

If there's one thing that you should learn early on about France and the French it's that they love their paperwork. If you're newly engaged, have decided to get married in Paris, and the forty-day residency issue is sorted out, the VERY first thing that you want to do is get the most recent list of required paperwork from the city hall (*mairie*) in which you plan to marry. Most of these documents have to be dated within specific time frames before being submitted, so it's important to get the list as soon as you can. It's important, though (and I can't stress this enough), that you get the official, most up-to-date list from the specific city hall in the district (*arrondissement*) in which you are planning to marry. The lists are essentially the same, but there could be slight variations from district to district, so to be on the safe side, you should probably go to the source. Here's a list of documents and information you'll be required to have:

⚜ Valid passport or a French residence permit (*carte de séjour*)

⚜ Birth certificate (*extrait d'acte de naissance*): Most city halls require that you present an original copy of a complete birth certificate (with full parentage details) along with a sworn translation, issued within three months of your requested wedding date. The translation must be done by a sworn translator (*traducteur assermente*), not merely someone who speaks French very well. A list of sworn translators is available in French city halls and your local French consulate or embassy.

⚜ Affidavit of law (*certificat de coutume*): This certifies that the American citizen is free to get married in France and that the marriage will be recognized in the United States.

⚜ Certificate of celibacy (*attestation tenant lieu de déclaration en vue de mariage ou de non remariage*): This is essentially the same thing as the *certificat de coutume*, a legal document that says you're free to marry. Some city halls require one of these documents over the other, and some require both. Be sure to clarify this with your specific city hall. Both of these documents must be dated less than three months from your wedding date.

⚜ Medical certificate (*certificat médical prénuptial*): You both must get a prenuptial medical certificate, which says that you were examined by a doctor *"en vue de mariage."* (Don't get nervous, girls. It's just a standard check-up, plus a couple of blood tests for things like rubella or toxoplasmosis). The marriage banns cannot be published until medical certificates have been submitted to the city hall. The certificates typically must be dated no earlier than two months before the publication of the banns. Any qualified doctor can perform the medical exam.

⚜ *Certificat du notaire*: If you're planning on having a prenuptial agreement, you must go through a lawyer who will provide you with a *certificat du notaire,* which you must submit to the city hall with the rest of your documents. It must have been drawn up no more than two months prior to the marriage. If there are no prenuptial contracts, then you'll be married under the *communauté réduites aux acquêts.* This means that what each of you owned personally before the marriage, or whatever comes to you afterwards through inheritance, remains your own, individual property. Only items or property that is acquired during the marriage is considered equally owned by both parties. (If you've ever seen or read Diane Johnson's *Le Divorce,* this scenario may look familiar to you.) If either of you were previously married, you must also provide a certified copy of the death certificate of the deceased spouse or a certified copy of the final divorce decree.

⚜ *Témoins*: In addition to all of the above, you will also have to choose and provide information on your witnesses (*témoins*)—two to four people who will act as your legal best men and/or maid(s) of honor—and sign the registry after the marriage ceremony. You will need to provide their names, addresses, professions and photocopies of their French identity cards or foreign passports with your dossier.

All of this needs to be presented, in person, to the mairie in time for them to check and approve your documents before posting the banns. They typically ask for your completed marriage file twenty days before their publication, but I usually suggest that my clients submit their file sooner than that, just in case there's a document missing. When all has been accepted and approved, you'll receive confirmation from the mairie of your wedding date (you can request a specific date and time when you drop off your paperwork, but they will assure you that nothing is confirmed until the dossier has been approved).

Keep in mind that *you must be legally married in a civil ceremony before you will be allowed to have a religious ceremony in France.* After your civil ceremony, you'll receive a *Livret de Famille*—a velvet booklet that contains your marriage certificate. It also has LOTS of extra pages for you to keep track of your future children. This little blue book is the Holy Grail. If you live in France, this book will make your administrative life here a lot easier pretty much until the day you die (in which your death will be noted in said little blue book). If you don't plan on staying in France, think of it as the ultimate wedding present.

Getting married in a foreign country is rarely easy. A Parisian wedding is just a bit more difficult than that. But if you are willing and able, the lasting memory of exchanging your vows beneath the shadow of the Eiffel Tower or in the cobbled halls of a centuries-old chateau is worth the few months of frustration.

FRENCH EMBASSY UNITED STATES
4101 Reservoir Road, NW
Washington, D.C. 20007
www.info-france-usa.org
www.ambafrance-us.org

FRENCH CONSULATES UNITED STATES
The Lenox Building, Suite 500
3399 Peachtree Road
Atlanta, Georgia 30326
www.consulfrance-atlanta.org

88 Kearny Street, Suite 600
San Francisco, California 94108
www.consulfrance-sanfrancisco.org

934 Fifth Avenue
New York, New York 10021
www.consulfrance-newyork.org

FRENCH EMBASSY ENGLAND
58 Knightsbridge
London SW1X 7JT
www.ambafrance-uk.org

FRENCH EMBASSY CANADA
42 Promenade Sussex
Ottawa, Ontario K1M 2C9
www.ambafrance-ca.org/

# How to Get Married in a Catholic Church in Paris

After "how can we get married on the Eiffel Tower," I would have to say that my second most requested Paris wedding venue inquiry would be "we want to get married at Notre Dame Cathedral." Unfortunately, unless you have friends or relatives in some *extremely* high places, it is next to impossible to marry in Notre Dame. I think it's also worthwhile to mention here that, for a foreigner legally living outside of France, it isn't exactly a cakewalk to get married in any church in Paris. One of the biggest things to keep in mind is that before a Catholic church in France will even *consider* marrying you, you must first have a civil ceremony either in France or in your home country. Once that is sorted, you should then put on your Sunday's best, and get thee to the church in question for a little face-time.

The tricky part is that in order to get married in a church in France, you have to get direct permission from the priest of the church, and, quite frankly, he may not want to do it. Keep in mind that France is a traditional Catholic country, and parishes are pretty deep-rooted in their communities. You are asking to be accepted into the folds of a parish in order to take part in a holy rite. If the priest feels that you aren't considerate of this, or feels that you're trying to "buy" a place in their church (I can't tell you how many American clients have contacted me asking for help after being denied permission to marry at a church after they've grossly waggled inch-thick stacks of fifties in the priest's face); he has every right to say no. So I suggest that, if you're able, you and your betrothed start going to the church for a while before you first meet with the priest—*and make sure that he sees you.* When you do have your first meeting with him, be as reverent and respectful as the meeting deserves, and be prepared to plead your case. I'll just tell you now that nine times out of ten, the priest will "strongly suggest" that you marry in your own parish, all while walking you out the front door! So get your elevator pitch ready. Let him know how much

France, Paris, and the arrondissement means to you, and why you *must* marry in *his* church. If you have any warm-n-fuzzy stories to tell (a grandparent or cousin who was married or buried in the church, for instance), be sure to get them in there. And, of course, a plate of killer homemade chocolate-chip cookies never hurt.

If you're planning to marry in a church in Paris but aren't currently in France, honestly, you have your work cut out for you. Your emails will more than likely go unanswered. If you try to phone the church directly, you will probably never make it past the church secretary. The best suggestion that I have is to find a friend or relative with strong, personal ties within that specific parish to make the plea on your behalf. This should be someone that you are on very good terms with, because it may require more than a few visits with the priest before you get your final answer.

And speaking of final answers, as anyone who has spent any time at all in France knows, the first answer is always *"non."* Just ignore that one and ask again in a different way. If, after the fourth or fifth try, the answer is *still* no, then I would suggest you move on to Plan B, a symbolic ceremony in a private chapel or maybe a blessing ceremony in a non-denominational Parisian church.

If you're lucky enough to have the right connections and are able to find a priest in France who agrees to perform your wedding ceremony in his church, you'll find that you still have to get your paperwork in order. Ah, paperwork—France just wouldn't be France without it. But no worries. Your American Wedding Planner in Paris comes through again! Here are the documents typically required to marry in a Catholic church in France. As with legal ceremony requirements, you must get the official list from your specific church in France, but here's what you can expect:

- ✤ A cover letter written on formal letterhead from your parish priest that gives you the "official" go-ahead to marry in a foreign country: The letter basically says that the priest knows you and that there is no reason that you shouldn't be able to marry in France. It should include the name of the French church that you'll be marrying in, as well as the date of the wedding. He needs to include your original Pre-Nuptial Inquiry form, which will then need to be stamped with an official seal from the bishop. Also, your priest will need to include a copy of a certificate proving that you have completed Pre-Cana classes.

- ✤ Another letter, also on formal letterhead, from the bishop of your parish: This letter pretty much says the same as the priest's letter. It gives the name of the French church, the wedding date and states that the bishop knows of no reason why you cannot marry in a Catholic church in France.

- ✤ Baptism and confirmation certificates (*un extrait d'acte de baptême*) that have been issued within six months of your wedding date: These certificates must also have the official seal from your bishop on them in order to be accepted by the church in France.

- ✤ Non-catholic people: If your spouse-to-be is not Catholic, then you'll need to send a completed and signed Permission for a Mixed Religion document. You can get this from your parish priest as well.

- ✤ Divorced people: If one or both of you have been divorced, you are not allowed to marry in a Catholic church in France unless an annulment has been granted. You will have to submit proof of this along with your documents.

- ✤ Your marriage certificate as proof of your civil ceremony: Remember, you can only be married in a Catholic church in France *after* you have had a civil ceremony.

All of the above documents need to be submitted to the priest of your French church at least two months before your wedding date in order to give you enough leeway in case there are any unforeseen hitches. As some of the documents are time sensitive, I typically suggest that you give yourself four to six months before your wedding date to start accumulating your documents. This is all *after* you have received confirmation directly from the priest that he will marry you in his church, of course.

Being married in one of the dozens of beautiful, historic churches of Paris is a chance of a lifetime. Although the process to get there may seem a bit daunting, the memory of your unforgettable Parisian celebration will make the journey worth it.

Eglise Catholique en France
http://www.eglise.catholique.fr/

The American Church in Paris
65 quai d'Orsay
75007 Paris
www.acparis.org/

# French Weddings vs. American Weddings

My husband and I were once at a wedding in France when, around 11:30 p.m., just as dessert was being served, a couple showed up and sat down at our table. I assumed that they were just terribly late (or terribly rude), but after chatting with them for a bit, I realized that I had already spoken to them earlier that day after the ceremony at the church. Apparently, they had then mysteriously disappeared for the following five hours. I mentioned this to my husband, and he casually remarked, "Oh, they must have just been invited for the dessert." Me: "Um, *WHAT?*" Lui: "Yeah, Jean-Luc only works with Philippe, so they were probably invited just for the dessert." Me (visibly taken aback): "And they *came*?" Lui: "Ouf! You Americans are *trop sensible* (too sensitive)!"

And that, for me, is one of the biggest cultural differences between American and French weddings. A typical American wedding is made up of a ceremony (civil, religious or symbolic), a cocktail hour and a lunch or dinner reception followed by dancing. The entire event is usually over by midnight at the latest. When you're invited to an American wedding, you're either invited to the ceremony and reception, or, as is the case when the ceremony venue is very small, just the reception. A typical French wedding, on the other hand, lasts all day AND leads into the next. It starts with a civil ceremony at a city hall in the morning, is followed by a religious ceremony in a place of worship if the couple chooses, and then a *vin d'honneur* (small cocktail reception), and then a bigger cocktail reception, followed by a four- or five-course meal, and then finally, dancing. The dancing often starts between dinner courses in order to give guests a chance to work up more of an appetite! A typical French wedding doesn't end until 3 or 4 a.m., or even later (there's even an old French custom that is still practiced in some families today, where vats of French onion soup are brought out to the remaining guests at around 5 or 6 in the morning!).

Now, here's the deal: Guests in France can be invited to all, or only *part* of a wedding's festivities, even JUST dessert around midnight, and they don't get offended by that! If you were to receive an invitation to a French wedding, it would probably say something like:

*M et Mme LeFrancais*
*ont le bonheur de vous annoncer le mariage de leurs enfants*
*Paul et Virginie*
*et ont le plaisir de vous inviter au mariage civil*
*ainsi qu'à la bénédiction nuptiale qui auront leiu*
*le samedi 2 décembre 2013 à 15 heures*
*en l'église St Paul de Vence*
*A l'issue de la cérémonie, un vin d'honneur sera servi*
*à la salle paroissiale . . .*

That's saying that you've been invited to the civil ceremony, the church ceremony and the *vin d'honneur* immediately following the church ceremony in a small reception room at the church. In a typical French wedding, pretty much everyone is invited to the above. Okay, this is where it gets a bit funky: *If* you're worthy, you will then have another card inserted into your invitation that says something like:

*Paul, Virginie et leurs parents espèrent votre présence au diner*
*qui aura lieu vers 20 heures au restaurant LaDida.*
*Réponse souhaitée avant le xxx.*

That means that you've been invited to the dinner, with dancing to follow. SCORE!

Or instead, you could receive a card that says something like:

*M et Mme LeFrancais de vous recevoir pour le dessert,*
*le 2 decembre 2013, à partir de 23 heure, à la salle de Trucmuche*

Which means that you've only been invited for dessert. Blam!

The reasoning is, of course, that everyone gets to participate in Paul and Virginie's joyous day, and La Famille LeFrancais isn't left with the financial burden of feeding the entire arrondissement. My hang-up is this: What if you *thought* you were a Level One, Cradle-to-the-Grave, Whole Enchilada-type of *belle amie*, but then, when you ripped open your invitation, OH SNAP—there was a cake card? What does that do to your friendship? How could you not be all frosty at the water-cooler the next time you see your "friend"? Wouldn't you think twice before you tucked that 20€ bill into your Former Favorite Niece's birthday card? How could you not spend the rest of the time before the wedding trying to dissect every conversation you've ever had in order to determine why you were "caked"?

I'm certainly not slamming French wedding etiquette. Like I said, French people don't seem to mind this at all. Now that I think about it, maybe it's not cultural at all. Maybe it's just my own insecurities? If you were French, would you be offended (okay, slightly miffed) if you received an invitation to a wedding ceremony and dessert, but not to the dinner? *Am I being "trop sensible"?*

# The Best Places to Propose in Paris

As a wedding planner in Paris, I can't tell you how many requests I get from panicked grooms-to-be looking for help on proposing to their bride-to-be at the top of the Eiffel Tower. One thing that I like to advise these guys is that a proposal, like *amour,* isn't just about the payoff. One Pretty Spot + Four Little Words + Two Months Salary may = *"oui,"* but if in the end all she remembers is the bling, you've wasted a lot of time and energy! No, a truly unforgettable proposal requires a little foreplay. If you've decided to propose in Paris, you need to set the scene and completely immerse your future *épouse* (bride) in the sights, sounds and sentiments of Paris. Sure, the top of the Eiffel Tower is amazingly impressive, but wading through the endless lines of tourists and panhandlers to get there does tend to take a bit of the shine off.

With this in mind, I've compiled the American Wedding Planner in Paris' Top Five Most Romantic Spots to Propose in Paris:

1. ILE DE LA CITÉ: The first spot on my list is the Ile de la Cité, the cradle of Parisian civilization, where the ancient Parisii tribe lived before the Romans conquered them in A.D. 57. If you're bringing your sweetie all the way to Paris to propose, what could be more romantically symbolic than proposing at the very epicenter of Paris? With beautiful monuments like Notre Dame Cathedral, the Pont Neuf, the Conciergerie and Sainte-Chapelle, sprinkled with little parks, squares and markets, it's one of the most romantic spots in Paris, with perfect "proposal ops" for both day and night.

2. JARDIN DU PALAIS ROYAL: This one is a more personal favorite. My French husband wooed me oh-so-many years ago with romantic walks through the Palais Royal. All of the elements of the perfect proposal are here.

  ❧ Mystery and Intrigue: The gardens are hidden from the street on all sides by almost identical buildings. You'll need a good map (or a little know-how) to find one of the doorways that enter onto the garden.

  ❧ Peace and Quiet: The same walls keep the noise of the Parisian traffic out. If you're lucky, there may be a cellist or opera singer performing beneath the tall arcades, but usually the loudest sound you'll hear will be coming from the beautiful fountain in the center of the garden.

  ❧ Romantic Ambiance: The arcades of the Palais Royal house cute little shops, restaurants and cafes—a perfect place to wander through, soaking up Parisian atmosphere before you stroll over to one of the benches that dot the park and ask for your honey's hand in marriage . . .

*If you've decided to propose in Paris, you need to set the scene and completely immerse your future bride in the sights, sounds and sentiments of Paris.*

3. PONT DES ARTS: How could she say no to a proposal on one of the most enchanting bridges in Paris? The Pont des Arts is a wooden pedestrian bridge, which leads to the Louvre and has the most amazing views of Paris (with the Eiffel Tower in the distance) and the Ile de la Cité. A little wine, a little *baguette et fromage* (bread and cheese), the sun setting on the Seine . . . and she's yours for the asking! And while you're there, don't forget to leave a Love Lock as a memento of your Parisian adventure. People write their initials on a lock, attach it to the bridge, make a wish, then throw the key into the river. There are love locks all over the world. The one in Paris is at Pont des Arts.

4. CANAL ST. MARTIN: This charming, tree-lined waterway in the 10th arrondissement is still pretty much overlooked by tourists, especially in off-peak months. Built by Napoleon III in 1825 to transport materials from quarries in the north to the Seine, the waterway's charming iron footbridges and locks are still standing, and set a romantic tone for a different type of wedding proposal. After checking out the "bohemian chic" shops and waterfront cafés along the Quais de Valmy and de Jenmapes, stroll on over to the Parc de la Villette and board a canal cruise. Take a tranquil two-hour ride down the canal and out onto the Seine, where you'll have plenty of opportunities to pop the question.

5. MAISON BLANCHE: Located on the top of an old Art Deco theater off the Champs-Elysées, Maison Blanche is a hip and trendy romantic restaurant where you go to see and be seen. Reserve a table near the windows if you want to impress her with a breath-taking panoramic view of Paris and the Eiffel Tower, or book one of the cozy booths if you want something a bit more *intime* (intimate) for the big moment.

# Top Five Tips for an Elopement or Vow-Renewal in Paris

There are tons of reasons why people choose to elope: to save money, to save time, to save their sanity! Couples who contact me about eloping in Paris also typically display a very strong romantic streak. Since I find myself answering a lot of the same questions week after week, and since the answers can easily apply to couples wanting to renew their vows as well, I've decided to compile the American Wedding Planner in Paris' Top Five Tips for Planning an Elopement or Vow-Renewal in Paris.

1. START PLANNING EARLY: Be aware that there aren't many English-speaking celebrants available in Paris, and most of them work full time at their own churches, which leaves a limited amount of time to officiate weddings for couples coming from overseas. To be fair, you should plan on contacting a celebrant at least three months in advance of your ceremony (longer if you're planning on eloping during the high season).

2. HIRE A GOOD WEDDING PLANNER: This one is pretty simple. A destination wedding is a destination wedding, whether it's just you two or two hundred of your closest friends! Besides having access to top-notch local vendors, hiring a wedding planner based in the destination that you're planning your elopement takes the pressure off you and your honey, and gives you time to concentrate on planning your honeymoon. As when you're hiring your officiant, keep in mind that most wedding planners need at least three months notice to book an elopement ceremony.

3. TRY NOT TO PLAN TOO MUCH: So, my first pointer was to start planning early, but that's not to say to plan every single second of your event! Remember, France runs at its own pace, and to most Americans, that's about three and a half paces behind the United States! I've had elopement clients send me their itineraries timed to the quarter hour, "Car Pick-Up at Hotel: 12:45. Arrive at Eiffel Tower: 1:05. Waiter brings first glass of champagne: 2:17, etc. etc." If you learn nothing else from this book, learn this: You can pay a deposit, fax an Excel spreadsheet, confirm, and re-confirm an order, but it won't really confirm anything. In Paris, "on time" typically means between fifteen and thirty-five minutes "late" by U.S. standards. So, just know that it <u>will</u> all work out in the end, and the wedding ceremony will be just as lovely twenty minutes "later" than planned.

4. YOU CANNOT GET MARRIED ON TOP OF THE EIFFEL TOWER: Let me just say that once again for the girls at the back: You Can NOT get married on top of the Eiffel Tower! The Eiffel Tower is a national monument. Occasionally, the top is rented out for corporate functions, but not to private individuals. If you want to host a small, personal event at the Eiffel Tower, you'll be encouraged to rent private rooms at one of the two restaurants in the tower.

5. THINK OFF THE BEATEN PATH: If you've already decided to elope to Paris, chances are you're a pretty non-traditional couple. So why settle for the "same-old same-old" once you've arrived in Paris? Sure, you can get married beneath the Eiffel Tower. It's gorgeous, historical, romantic—everything that you could ask from a wedding in Paris. But wouldn't it be really cool to exchange your vows on top of the Parc des Buttes Chaumont, with its amazing panoramic view of the city spread out at your feet? Or even at sundown in the dramatic shadows of the Pyramide du Louvre? Since you're creating your own unique elopement ceremony, the world (or at least Paris) is your oyster! Elopement ceremonies tend to be fairly short, so if you're mindful of the legalities of your intended venue (no standing on the grass, for example, if you're not permitted to do so), and respectful of your environment (e.g., don't hire an accordionist to serenade you in a busy restaurant), your elopement in Paris should go off without a hitch!

# What to Wear to a Wedding in Paris

You've just received an invitation to your first French wedding. Your initial thought ("How exciting!") is quickly replaced by, "OMG, what am I going to wear?" Fear not, your American Wedding Planner in Paris is here to guide you. First, you should know that people in France don't typically tend to dress up for weddings as much as they do in the States. At Franco-American weddings, you can always pick out the American guests by their clothes and their smiles. I, personally, find this absolutely refreshing, I mean, if you can't dress up for a wedding, when can you dress up? This isn't to say that the French never dress for weddings. It's just that sometimes the look tends to be more Casual Friday than Friday Night Swanky. If the wedding is between families of a certain background, of course, you will dress up. Unfortunately, in many destination wedding situations you only know one-half of the couple, and don't know anything about his or her family's background.

So how do you decide what to wear? The most obvious clue is the invitation. Is it a classic cream or ivory card stock with formal text and titles? Or is it a more contemporary design, with a touch of color and modern text? A formal invitation doesn't always mean a formal wedding, but it's a pretty good clue.

The second hint is the address of the city hall, church and/or reception. Like most places, there are tonier sides and less tonier sides of every town in France. If the wedding is in Paris, and is being held in the mairie and church in the 16th arrondissement with the reception at the Hotel Crillon, it's safe to say that you should dress up. If the civil ceremony takes place in the city hall of the 13th arrondissement, with no church ceremony but a reception dinner cruise on the Seine, then you will probably be more comfortable in a more casual outfit.

One important bit of information to know is that when you're shopping for your French wedding outfit, you're actually shopping for two outfits! Like I've mentioned before, French weddings last all day long, and most guests will

change outfits sometime between the morning ceremony and evening reception, with the evening look typically more casual than the morning's. Again, look to the location of the venue to help you with this.

So, just how "dressy" and how "casual" is acceptable at a French wedding? For a standard formal French wedding ceremony, think "Four Weddings and a Funeral," but a little less "British madness" with the hat. A beautiful day suit or ensemble by Catherine Varnier, for example, with or without a stylish chapeau should do the trick. Try Les Chapeaux de Béa in Paris for a gorgeous selection of wedding hats. For a more casual wedding, a chic and classic look by Tara Jarmon paired with trendy bold accessories should help you fit right in with the rest of the Parisian *invités* (guests).

If you plan to attend the religious ceremony, be aware that it is a respectful gesture for women to cover their shoulders in church. So if you choose a sleeveless number, be sure to bring a jacket or pashmina with you for the ceremony. Also, in France, as in the United States, it is typically *interdit* (forbidden) for any woman other than the bride to wear white.

Many French wedding magazines and websites will have sections devoted to clothes and accessories for the wedding guests. Called *tenues d'invités* in French. Check out www.Madame.LeFigaro.fr for a great list that is updated often.

CATHERINE VARNIER
48, rue d'Assas
75006 Paris
01 42 84 15 12
www.catherine-varnier.com

TARA JARMON
73, avenue Champs-Elysées 75008
www.tarajarmon.com

LES CHAPEAUX DE BÉA
www.leschapeauxdebea.com

With French weddings lasting *all day* and into the next morning, many guests will *change outfits* sometime between the morning ceremony and evening reception.

# MELISSA & MICHAEL

Paris is brimming with hundreds of *breathtaking*,

romantic locations. Why not consider

exchanging vows beneath the echoing,

*vaulted ceilings* of the Place des Vosges?

For their Parisian elopement, Melissa and Michael wanted to not only celebrate their marriage, but they also wanted to celebrate Paris—in all of its stylish glory. So we organized a whirlwind, citywide photo session following their intimate ceremony at the base of the Eiffel Tower. It was chic and simple, with a hearty helping of Parisian glamour.

WEDDING DESIGN AND COORDINATION
Kim Petyt, Parisian Events
www.parisianevents.com

PHOTOGRAPHY
Milos and Natasa Horvat
www.miloshorvat.com

HAIR AND MAKEUP
James
www.jmsbyjames.com

DRESS
White by Vera Wang

BOOTS
Ralph Lauren Paris
vintage army issue

HAIR ACCESSORY
Tessa Kim
www.tessakim.com

GROOM
Paul Smith from head to toe;
suit, shirt, tie, cufflinks, socks,
shoes and belt

WEDDING BANDS
Alan Friedman of Beverly Hills
www.alandiamonds.com

# Marie Antoinette Moderne

❧ PARISIAN COLOR PALETTE: Pink champagne, dusty rose, and gilded gold paired with mercury and hand-blown glass

THE LOOK FOR A MARIE ANTOINETTE—INSPIRED EVENT CAN BE DESCRIBED AS CHATEAU DE VERSAILLES, SUMPTUOUS YET INTIMATE, DELICATE, LUMINOUS, FEMININE AND ELEGANT. THIS STYLE IS AN HOMAGE TO MARIE ANTOINETTE AND HER LAVISH EXCESSES, SIMPLIFIED TO JUST THE ESSENTIAL EXQUISITE DETAILS.

DESIGN AND STYLING
Kim Petyt
Parisian Events
www.parisianevents.com

PHOTOGRAPHY
Ian Holmes
www.ianholmes.net

MENUS
CT Designs Calligraphy
www.ct-designs.com

VENUE
Maceo Restaurant
www.maceorestaurant.com

CAKE
Sugarplum Cake Shop
www.sugarplumcakeshop.com

FLOWERS
Atelier Lieu-Dit
www.lieu-dit-paris.fr

# Tête à Tête with Wedding Dress Designer Ana Quasoar

Walking into Ana Quasoar's showroom in the 2nd arrondissement of Paris is like stepping through Alice's looking glass. All at once, you're transported from the bustling streets of Paris into a magical world full of cherubs and fairies, princesses and queens. Her ethereal designs carry you across lands and through time, with Ana playing Scheherazade, Perrault and the White Rabbit all rolled into one.

**Parisian Party**: Where do you find your inspiration?

**Ana Quasoar**: My inspirations are diverse. When I was a child, I used to love to read fairytales and legends, and so I'm full of tales from all over the world—Japan, South America, Greek mythology—all of these stories give me inspiration. For instance, I was thinking about a fairytale about a beautiful princess who goes to a ball, and as she dances, flowers, pearls and precious stones fall from her dress. So I designed this dress like a cornucopia. And when a girl walks in it, she is literally floating. I'm a storyteller. Each dress that I create has its own story. I never tell the story to

clients in words, though, but when they put on one of my dresses, the story comes to life.

**Parisian Party**: Who are your clients? Is there a typical Ana Quasoar client?

**Ana Quasoar**: I have clients from twenty-one to sixty years old! Some are choosing dresses for their second wedding or are mothers of the bride. My clients are very, very different from each other. I have clients that are feminine and sexy and others who are sporty and natural. Far from each other, but they all want the same thing—a high-quality gown that represents who they are.

You know, we women are full of contradictions. This is what gives us our charm. That's what I love about women. They play on so many different levels all the time. In the morning, a woman may take her children to school, then she goes to work, then maybe she goes to a party after work, playing so many roles throughout one day. For me, a woman in her wedding gown must express at least two or three aspects of herself. We enhance two or three of these aspects to make her feel like a star on her wedding day, but a star that looks like herself. I'm not here to change a woman's image. I'm here to supplement, to enhance who she already is.

**Parisian Party**: Vera Wang has been credited with revolutionizing the modern American bride. Who do you think has played a part in influencing the current French wedding style?

**Ana Quasoar**: I think before Max Chaoul, the scene around wedding dresses in France was very boring. But then Max Chaoul arrived and he had such an impact with his crazy scenarios. We have very different styles of designing, but I do recognize that he is someone who really shook up the wedding scene in France. There is also Delphine Manivet. She expresses something that, again, is different from my own universe, but is still very authentic and responding to a need. They are very opposite, but for me, they are shaking it up a bit. Max brings a sense of fun and craziness, and Delphine brings a down-to-earth, relaxed style, and I think I'm more baroque and pure—in between the two, I imagine. But we are all passionate about what we do.

**Parisian Party**: All around the world, brides dream of coming to Paris to buy their wedding gowns. Can you describe a little bit about the experience that a bride would have purchasing an Ana Quasoar gown?

**Ana Quasoar**: We have clients coming from all over the world. Some come in with a file of photos and notes and they know exactly what they want. Some come with a drawing that they've made, and we'll talk a bit, then I'll go over and select a gown from my collection and they'll tell me that its exactly how they imagined their dress! Some girls have no idea at all and are nervous. My role then is to make a shelter for them, and to help them to really discover what part of themselves that they want to put out there on display.

If a client isn't living in France, we really try to arrange the fittings around the bride's schedule. Typically, we will need two or three visits. If she comes in, has a *coup de coeur* (instantly falls in love) with one of my gowns, we'll take her measurements and can have her toile within a few days. Then the next visit will be the fitting with the unfinished dress, and if it's possible for her to stay in Paris for a few days, then we can usually complete the dress after that fitting. This of course depends on how detailed the dress is. Normally, the entire process takes a few months, but it also depends on the time of year.

Even though we ship worldwide, most brides want to come and pick up the finished dress themselves. One thing that I like to do before she leaves is to council her on the whole story—how she will walk in the dress and what style of bouquet would best suit her in her gown, all the details that will make her feel the most comfortable. All brides have their own personal story that I try to help them express on their wedding day. It's not just about selling the gown, it's like a piece of jewelry or a perfume that has been created. It's not just a dress but also the image of the person that I'm creating.

Ana Quasoar
7, rue Banque 75002
www.anaquasoar.com

# The French Croquembouche: Let Them Eat Cake

One of the things that I like the most about designing American weddings in Paris is coming up with interesting ways to mix the two cultures. With a little bit of creativity, I've found that a lot of the ideas work just as well for a Paris-themed wedding or event held outside of France. For instance, one of the ways that I like to suggest that my clients add a touch of Parisian drama to their wedding is by serving a traditional French wedding cake—a croquembouche instead of the classic multi-tiered American cake for dessert.

The croquembouche is a tower of cream-filled, puff-pastry balls (called *choux* in French) that are piled into a high pyramid and encircled with caramelized sugar. This sugar is what gives the dessert its name—croquembouche loosely translates to "crunch in the mouth." In addition to spun sugar, the croquembouche can be decorated with icing, chocolate, sugared almonds or candy ribbons. In France, any patisserie worth its weight in salt will be able to help you obtain a croquembouche. One of the most fabulous Parisian patisseries is Ladurée, which is known around the world for its macaron. Ladurée also creates beautiful croquembouche towers in either plain choux drizzled in caramelized sugar or covered in sugar icing in its signature pastel colors. Ladurée offers a wide selection of crème flavors like vanilla, pistachio, caramel, rose and orange blossom. The most popular among Parisian brides, they tell me, is the vanilla-bourbon cream, which has just a slight touch of aged rum.

Now, one of the highlights of a French wedding is the presentation of Le Gâteau (the cake). Unlike in traditional American weddings where the cake is on display as a focal point throughout the entire reception dinner, a French wedding cake is brought out at dessert time, usually with a lot of hoopla. A typical serving of croquembouche is around three or four choux per guest. So, at a wedding of 100 guests, you can imagine the height of some of these cakes. When it's time to present the croquembouche, the lights will go down, and the DJ will start the guests chanting, "Le gateau! Le gateau!" Amid quite a bit of fanfare (think "Rocky's Theme" or "2001 Space Odyssey"), the head chef and his assistants will bring out the cake to the happy couple. As if a three-and-a-half-foot tower of cream-filled puff pastries dripping in caramelized spun sugar isn't enough, the cake at a French wedding is also presented with fireworks shooting out from all over it. No joke! After the flames die down, the couple then breaks off a few of the choux and eats them. The cake is then whisked away to be cut, plated and served to guests.

Ask your local French bakery about creating a croquembouche for your French-inspired wedding reception. For those concerned with fire codes, try substituting individual sparklers for the fireworks. Pass them out to guests before the dessert and let them know to light them at the designated time.

LENÔTRE
10, Champs-Elysées
75008 Paris, France
www.lenotre.com

FAUCHON
24-26-30, place de la Madeleine
75008 Paris, France
www.fauchon.com

CROQUEMBOUCHE
OUTSIDE OF FRANCE

GERHARD MICHLER
950 Illinois Street
San Francisco, California 94107
(415) 255-1128
www.gerhardmichler.com

CECI CELA PATISSERIE
55 Spring Street
New York, New York 10012
(212) 274-9179
www.cecicelanyc.com/le

PAPILLON PATISSERIE
Unit 66B The Peacocks Centre
Woking, Surrey, GU21 6GB
Great Britain
www.lepapillonpatisserie.com

CROQUEMBOUCHE PATISSERIE
1635 Botany Road
Botany, New South Wales 2019
Australia
www.croquembouche.com.au

*Caramelized sugar* is what gives

the dessert its name—croquembouche

loosely translates to "*crunch in the mouth.*"

# FAVOR IDEAS FOR A
# MARIE ANTOINETTE–THEMED WEDDING

If you're looking for ways to bring a little empire-chic into your Parisian wedding, look no further than the Marie Antoinette–inspired gift line available through La Réunion des Musées Nationaux. The collection, made up of fashion and tabletop accessories, small desk items, books, games and DVDs, has something for every member of your bridal party. For the mothers of the bride and groom, an heirloom-worthy brooch shaped in the queen's initials (which can be seen on the balustrade of the staircase at The Petit Trianon) is available. Bridesmaids will love the pear-shaped, crystal-drop earrings by Lalique, which were inspired by a pair of earrings worn by the queen in a painting created in 1787 by Louise-Elisabeth Vigée-Le-Brun. And for the boys in your entourage, how about a "Marie Antoinette et les Disciples de Loki" game for their Nintendo DS? All are available through the Boutiques de Musées: www.boutiquesdemusees.fr.

MUSÉE DU LOUVRE
75001 PARIS, FRANCE

MUSÉE DE L'ORANGERIE
JARDIN DES TUILERIES
75001 PARIS, FRANCE

MUSÉE CARNAVALET—
HISTOIRE DE PARIS
23, RUE DE SÉVIGNÉ
75003 PARIS, FRANCE

MUSÉE PICASSO
5, RUE DE THORIGNY
75003 PARIS, FRANCE

MUSÉE EUGÈNE DELACROIX
6, RUE DE FURSTENBERG
75006 PARIS, FRANCE

GALERIES NATIONALES,
GRAND PALAIS
AVENUE DU GÉNÉRAL EISENHOWER
75008 PARIS, FRANCE

# A VISIT TO LADURÉE

For the meager few who still don't know about the magic of the macaron, let me explain it to you: macarons are two small, airy, almond-based cookies held together by either a ganache, butter cream or jam filling. Originally a simple almond cookie, it wasn't until the 1900s that it became the colorful, Frenchy treat that everyone is talking about. That was when Pierre Desfontaines had the brilliant idea to color, flavor and sandwich macarons and then sell them in his little Parisian shop called Ladurée.

Ah, Ladurée—for lovers of Paris, lovers of macarons, and lovers of LOVE around the world—Ladurée is Shangri-La. Like her first pair of heels or her first kiss, a girl never forgets her first visit to Ladurée. Mine was during an early trip to Paris. I was walking along the Champs-Elysées and noticed a long line of people weaving out from the entrance of a gilded gold-and-pistachio-colored storefront. At that moment, it was as if fate took over. Wherever I was heading that day instantly dropped out of my mind as my soul got in line to enter Ladurée, with my body instinctively following.

From the first crispy crunch to the cool, creamy finale—only two bites—of that macaron, I knew that my life was changed forever. Since then, I've been a *fidéle maîtresse* (faithful mistress) to Ladurée macarons, tempted by the likes of Pierre Hermé and Dalloyau, but rarely straying.

As a wedding planner in Paris, I've lovingly guided clients through Ladurée's assortment of macaron for their famous *piéce montée*—the tall, conical tower of multi-colored, multi-flavored macarons that they first invented for weddings and celebrations; through flavors like cassis, violette, fleur d'oranger, caramel au beurre salé and beyond. I've squealed with joy as couples have chosen to privatize one of Ladurée Champs-Elysées luxurious salons to host their macaron-filled rehearsal dinner or day-after brunch. I've choked back tears of pride as Ladurée has expanded to the four corners of the globe, creating custom macaron flavors like cinnamon-raisin for the New York market or coffee-cardamom for Beirut, along the way.

Sometimes I wonder what I'd do if I ever lost my lovely Ladurée. I guess if that day ever came, I'd pick myself up and find some other way to "get my macaron on." Lucky for me, the macaron craze has spread around the world, and can now be found in most major cities. After all, a Parisian wedding just isn't a Parisian wedding without macarons.

LADURÉE
75, Champs-Elysées
75008 Paris, France
www.laduree.fr

## MACARONS OUTSIDE OF FRANCE

LADURÉE
864 Madison Avenue
New York, New York 10021
www.laduree.fr

HONORÉ BAKERY
1413 NW 70th Street
Seattle, Washington 98117
www.honorebakery.com/

MYATT CAFÉ AND CHOCOLATIER
Shop 6244, V&A Waterfront
Cape Town, South Africa
www.myattcafe.com

BOUGIE MACARON & TEA
3 Russell Street, WC2B 5JD
London, United Kingdom
www.bougie.co.uk

# French Wedding Tradition: Lily of the Valley

May 1 is Labour Day in France and is also when the French celebrate spring by offering small sprigs of lilies of the valley as a good luck charm to those who hold a special place in their hearts. Since May 1 is the only time of the year when people can sell flowers on the street without having to buy a permit, all over Paris, people sell little bunches of lilies of the valley for a euro or two.

This sweet French custom started during the sixteenth century. Wedding banns were posted at the beginning of May, and wreaths of lily of the valley were hung in the doorways of the brides-to-be. During his reign, Charles IX also began offering sprigs of the flower for luck. As it happened, in the late 1800s, the international workers movement declared the first of May as May Day, in honor of the workers of the world. In France, workers and their supporters wore lily of the valley boutonnières on May 1. These days, French tradition says that you must offer at least one sprig of lily of the valley to loved ones on May Day. In the Victorian language of flowers, by the way, lily of the valley signified the return of happiness.

For a spring or summer wedding, what better way to incorporate this French tradition into your wedding than by adding some touches of lilies of the valley?

If you'd like to add a French touch to your lily of the valley wedding, try offering your guests boxes of muguet-flavored macarons from Ladurée or your bridesmaids bottles of muguet-scented perfume by Annick Goutal.

ANNICK GOUTAL
14, rue de Castiglione
75001 Paris, France
www.annickgoutal.com

# French Fashion for Children in Your Wedding

I remember this one time back when I was still living in the United States but was in France planning my wedding, and had a big "bridezilla" meltdown in the middle of a florist's shop. I didn't speak a word of French, and I couldn't get the florist to understand what I meant by "bridesmaid bouquets." The man kept shaking his head and showing me pictures of tiny little Barbie-sized bouquets in a catalog, bigger than a boutonnière, but more elaborate than a corsage. I had no idea WHY he kept showing me those. If I had only known then that "bridesmaids" don't exist in France, I would have thought ahead and brought a photo with me. Who knew?

In France, a traditional wedding is often made up of the bridal couple and parents, the couple's witnesses (the French equivalent of a maid of honor or best man, but with more paperwork involved), and anywhere from two to six (or more) small children. There are usually two girls or boys (called *demoiselles* or *garçons d'honneur*) who, during the processional, enter just before the bride and her father and act as flower girls or ring bearers. The rest of the children enter after the bride and will either assist with her train and/or veil or simply march behind her, often carrying tiny baskets of petals or nosegay bouquets. After the ceremony, the children exit before the couple, normally sprinkling rose petals or tiny paper hearts along the path as they go.

Now if you want to see cute, you've got to see a bunch of little French kids all decked out in their cortege ensembles. The outfits will typically match, with variations made for boys or girls. The girls' dresses will have a full skirt with a sash around the waste and a big bow at the back. The girls also will often have a ring of flowers around their hair. The boys normally will wear sort of a "Little Lord Fauntleroy" look—short pants or bloomers, page-boy collar and either no hat or a little floppy beret-type hat.

If you'd like to incorporate this French tradition into your wedding, there are tons of French labels and designers specializing in wedding attire. In Paris, Séverine Corneille in the 6th arrondissement has the most beautiful ensembles starting at 85€ (roughly around $110 USD) for a custom-made outfit. Ivoy Paris also has sweet, handmade wedding designs for children. Their showroom is also in the 6th, and select pieces are also sold at Le Bon Marché. In Paris, most department stores will carry ensembles in their bridal department. For more moderately priced outfits, take a look at online resources like Verbaudet or Cyrillus. They usually have a small collection of ceremony outfits for children for the spring and summer seasons.

SÉVERINE CORNEILLE
19, rue Jacob
75006 Paris, France
www.severine-corneille.com

IVOY PARIS
133, rue de Sèvres
75006 Paris, France
www.ivoyparis.com

LE BON MARCHÉ
24, rue de Sèvres
75007 Paris, France
www.lebonmarche.com

VERBAUDET
www.verbaudet.com

CYRILLUS
www.cyrillus.com

If fluffy, pink frou frou isn't exactly your style, that doesn't mean your wedding celebration can't still get the royal treatment. Remember, Marie Antoinette was also considered to be a bit of a rebel in her day. Tap into your inner *enfant terrible* (troublesome child) and create a Marie Antoinette—inspired wedding with hip, offbeat, "Rock and Royal" inspirations!

While Marie Antoinette may be known for her excesses, paring down to a few elegant details allows for the appearance of opulence, all while saving some funds. From a dramatic focal point like a venue's fabulous chandelier, to wedding favors found in the gift shop of Versailles itself, well-chosen design elements create flair that packs a punch.

WEDDING DESIGN AND COORDINATION
Kim Petyt
Parisian Events
www.parisianevents.com

PHOTOGRAPHY
One and Only Paris
www.oneandonlyparis
photography.com

VENUE
Salon des Miroirs, Paris

DRESS
Pronovias
www.pronovias.com

HAIR FASCINATOR
Cherry Chau
www.cherrychau.com

GROOM'S SUITING
Carven
www.carven.fr

CAKE
Sugarplum Cake Shop
www.sugarplumcakeshop.com

# Un Mariage Vert: Green Wedding in Paris

* INSPIRATION: Parisian country, fragrant, delicate, heartwarming, effortless; a French impressionist's picnic in the Parisian countryside, the perfect fit for those in love with simplicity and nature's quiet beauty

* PARISIAN COLOR PALETTE: A natural palette accentuated with iris blue, violet, French lavender and whimsical touches of gold leafing

OVER THE PAST FEW YEARS, GREEN WEDDINGS HAVE QUICKLY GONE FROM QUIRKY TREND TO ESTABLISHED NORM AS TODAY'S COUPLES REALIZE THAT IT IS POSSIBLE TO HAVE A CHIC, TRENDY WEDDING THAT'S BOTH AFFORDABLE AND ECO AND SOCIALLY RESPONSIBLE. BOOKS, BLOGS AND MAGAZINES HAVE POPPED UP ALL OVER THE GLOBE WITH INFORMATION AND INSPIRATION ON PLANNING GREEN CELEBRATIONS.

The world looks to Paris before choosing its trends, and these days the trend is towards sustainable durability. While "eco-friendly" might not be the first thought that comes to mind when you think Paris, the City of Lights is making great strides to modify that image. I've lived in Paris for more than ten years now and have found that, although France was a bit slow to jump on the "green" bandwagon, it has stepped up its pace over the past few years and now embraces the "ecolo-chic" trend with open arms. Whereas a few years ago, organic products in Paris had been relegated to a few dusty "dietary needs" shelves and fair trade items could only be found online or in a handful of out-of-the-way specialty stores.

Eco-conscious Parisians can now be found zipping around the city on *vélibs* (the city-wide public bicycle rental program), dashing into Natralia or Biocoop (Paris-wide organic grocery store chains) or heading over to shop for furniture, clothes or gifts in neighborhoods like the Marias or Montmartre with their clusters of trendy and eco-friendly specialty boutiques. *Les mariage verts* (green weddings) have built up momentum as well, and more and more Paris-based artisans are beginning to realize that today's engaged couples are not only looking for style, quality and value from their wedding vendors but also for a level of global or social responsibility as well.

VILLA DU LAC

DESIGN AND STYLING
Kim Petyt, Parisian Events
www.parisianevents.com

PHOTOGRAPHY
Ian Holmes
www.ianholmes.net

FLOWERS
Atelier Lieu-Dit
www.lieu-dit-paris.fr

INVITATION
Paper + Cup
www.papercupdesign.com

CAKES
Sugarplum Cake Shop
www.sugarplumcakeshop.com

# Top Five Ideas for a Green Parisian Wedding

So you and your trend-setting betrothed have decided to have a destination wedding. More than that, you've decided on a green destination wedding. You've e-mailed or hand delivered your recycled paper invitations. You've registered with World Wildlife Fund Weddings and Celebrations rather than your local Meat Hooks, Marbles & More. You've even offset the amount of carbon emissions used to fly you and your guests to Paris by donating money to help build wind turbines in India. But why should your eco-wedding stop there? A lot of people feel that planning a regular destination wedding is hard enough. The thought of trying to make it eco-friendly as well is just too much. In fact, with a locally based wedding planner and a little time online, you'll find that there are plenty of ways that you can incorporate green or eco-conscious elements into a destination wedding. For instance, at right are my top five ideas for a green or eco-friendly wedding in Paris.

⚜ Purchase or have a wedding dress custom created that uses all-natural, earth-friendly fibers. Elsa Gary is a French designer whose natural bridal collections include materials like silk, bamboo, hemp, soya and maize.

⚜ Have your wedding meal prepared by an organic French caterer. Ethiques et Toques is an organic catering company servicing Paris, Lyon and Blois.

⚜ Rather than tossing birdseed or blowing bubbles at the end of your ceremony, why not follow a wedding tradition from the South of France and have your guests shower you with handfuls of lavender, like those sold in packets from www.pluie-de-lavande.com?

⚜ Thank your guests with a sweet French wedding favor: a little sachet of organic hard candy or lollipops from La Butinerie.

⚜ Toast your nuptials with a glass of organic champagne: Jean-Pierre Fleury and Larmandier-Bernier are two to try.

WORLD WILDLIFE FUND WEDDINGS AND CELEBRATIONS
wwf.worldwildlife.org

ELSA GARY
30, boulevard du Temple
75011 Paris, France
www.elsagary.fr

ORGANIC CATERER

ETHIQUES ET TOQUES
40, Avenue Hoche
75008 Paris, France
www.ethique-et-toques.com

PLUIE DE LAVANDE
www.pluie-de-lavande.com

ORGANIC CANDY

LA BUTINERIE
www.confiserie-biologique.com

ORGANIC CHAMPAGNE

JEAN-PIERRE FLEURY
177, rue Saint-Denis
75002 Paris, France
www.champagne-fleury.fr

LARMANDIER-BERNIER
www.larmandier.com

# Rent a Parisian Wedding
# Dress: Graine de Coton

If you're planning a trip to Paris, and are tossing around the idea of an impromptu wedding or vow-renewal ceremony while you're there, I've got a great resource for you: Graine de Coton is a sweet little boutique in the 15th arrondissement where you can buy or rent a wedding dress at a fraction of its retail price. Sourcing items from individuals, workshops or end-of-stock bridal boutiques, the shop also rents gently owned bridesmaids, flower girl and ring bearer outfits and accessories. And for the last-minute "bride's best friend," witness or guest, the shop carries a nice selection of evening and party dresses too. Keep in mind that besides being affordable and practical, a pre-owned wedding dress is a great eco-friendly option for a green wedding in Paris.

GRAINE DE COTON
18, rue de l'Abbé Groult
75015 Paris, France
www.graine-de-coton.com

# A Luxury and Eco-Friendly Hotel in Paris

Here's a tip for eco-friendly couples planning an eco-fabulous honeymoon or romantic getaway in Paris. Sitting at the nexus of the Triangle d'Or in Paris, the luxurious five-star Hotel Fouquet's Barrière has become one of the most environmentally friendly hotels in the world. A member of the Leading Hotels of the World, Fouquet's Barrière is also one of the rare hotels to be Leading Green Certified. Its commitment to Dignified Luxury is supported even further by its triple-threat ISO certifications: for environmental initiatives, respectfulness towards human rights and the rights of children, and for its superior quality of service. In July 2010, Hotel Fouquet's Barrière was the first hotel in Europe to receive the distinguished Luxury Eco Certification Standard (L.E.C.S.) from Sustainable Travel International.

At Hotel Fouquet's Barrière, eco-conscious new-lyweds can reserve their stay through the hotel's Make a Carbon Neutral Booking program, which allows clients the opportunity to fully offset the carbon emissions generated by their travel. Once in Paris, couples can dine on bio ("organic" in French) produce at Le Diane, the hotel's gourmet restaurant, sip organic Pop Earth champagne (Pommery's first "eco-citizen" champagne that is made from grapes harvested from sustainable vineyards, bottled in lighter bottles that use only half the glass and labeled with recycled paper and printed with solvent-free inks), enjoy fair trade flowers and fruit juices in the hotel's U-Spa, or whisk around the city in one of the hotel's electric E Solex bikes or hybrid limousines. It's all part of what Fouquet's Barrière calls Dignified Luxury—living in an environmentally friendly manner while focusing on environmental issues.

HOTEL FOUQUET'S BARRIÈRE
46, avenue George V
75008 Paris, France
www.fouquets-barriere.com/

## VÉLIB BIKE RENTAL

Since 2007, the city of Paris has overseen an eco-friendly, self-service bike rental system called Vélib (*vélo* = bike, *liberté* = freedom). Available 24/7, Vélib has thousands of bikes and hundreds of pick-up and drop-off stations throughout Paris, where users can either rent the bikes on a daily, weekly or yearly basis. Since users can drop off bikes at any rental point rather than return to the spot where they initially pick them up, this is a great way for couples to get around while discovering Paris from aboveground. They can take in an exhibit and stop for a picnic in between, for example—all without having to worry about navigating the metro or contributing to the noise and air pollution of the Parisian streets.

VÉLIB
www.velib.paris.fr

# DIY FRENCH WEDDING FAVOR:
## LAVENDER SUGAR

Here is a simple, inexpensive DIY favor idea for a French-themed wedding or party: homemade *sucre de lavande*—lavender sugar. Some of the finest lavender and lavender-infused products come from the South of France, where lavender is used throughout daily life. Not only is it used to scent the home (dried in sachets or in distilled water for perfuming linens) and in soaps and creams, but it's also delicious in cooking. On cookies, cakes or fresh fruit, a sprinkling of lavender sugar is a great way to add a delicate French flavor to any dessert.

To make sucre de lavande, fill a large (depending on the number of favors you're making) sealable container with granular sugar. Add several sprigs or handfuls of dried lavender blossoms. Seal the container and let it sit for two weeks, shaking the container occasionally to mix evenly. When ready, pour the sugar through a sifter to get the blossoms out, or whirl the sugar and blossoms together through a mixer or coffee grinder. Fill small apothecary jars with the sugar, and add a recipe or two along with the gift tag, *et voilà*! DIY doesn't get much easier than this.

# MICHELLE & GUY

This is a regal, romantic wedding in the woods just outside of Paris. A palette of glacier gray, moss green and blush pink with pops of vibrant magenta are set against a Ray Charles soundtrack. We blended classic, traditional *champêtre* (bucolic) elements of the Parisian countryside where Michelle and Guy first fell in love, with the soulful sounds from their childhood—and left their guests *à bout de souffle* (breathless).

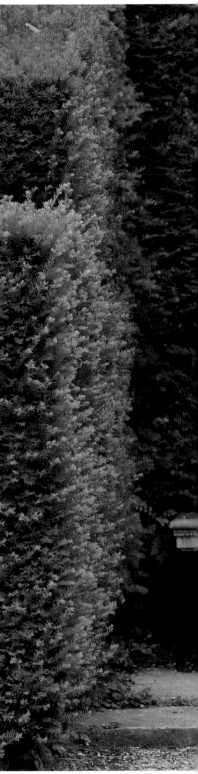

WEDGING DESIGN AND COORDINATION
Kim Petyt
Parisian Events
www.parisianevents.com

PHOTOGRAPHY
Arman Molavi
www.armanimage.com

VENUE
Jardin des Bagatelles

DRESS
Monique Lhuillier
www.moniquelhuillier.com

INVITATION SUITE
Hello Lucky
www.hellolucky.com

# Montmartre Mariage

❧ PARISIAN COLOR PALETTE: Black, anthracite and antique white, mercury glass and absinthe green

A TOUCH OF MONTMARTRE STYLE CAN BE TAKEN FROM PARIS DURING THE BELLE ÉPOQUE. THINK RENOIR AND TOULOUSE-LAUTREC AT THE MOULIN ROUGE. THIS LOOK IS VINTAGE AND SENSUAL, A ROMANTIC TRIBUTE TO THE VIVACIOUS, BOHEMIAN NEIGHBORHOOD KNOWN FOR ITS MUSIC HALLS, ABSINTHE DRINKERS AND THE FILM *AMÉLIE POULAIN*.

VENUE
Private home

DESIGN AND STYLING
Kim Petyt, Parisian Events
www.parisianevents.com

PHOTOGRAPHY
Ian Holmes
www.ianholmes.net

FLOWERS
Atelier Lieu-Dit
www.lieu-dit-paris.fr

LETTERPRESSED MENU
Paper + Cup
www.papercupdesign.com

CAKE
Sugarplum Cake Shop
www.sugarplumcakeshop.com

# Tête à Tête with Paris Corset Designer Loanna Haseltine

Although an early version can be traced back as far as 2000 BC, the saucy undergarment that we now know as the corset didn't become popular until the fifteenth century. It was then, legend has it, that the queen of France, Catherine de Medici, banned "thick waists" from her court. She supposedly had an iron corset designed that she would force any lady in her court that couldn't wrap both hands around her waist to wear.

Through the centuries that followed, as fashion evolved, corsets evolved, ditching the iron for lace, and incorporated ivory or whalebone "busks" that cinched in the waists and elongated women's shapes. By the late nineteenth century, corsets were a mainstay for women around the world, including the women of the Paris *Belle Époque,* as depicted by the corseted *bourgeoisie* ladies in Manet's *Jardin des Tuileries* as well as the tawdry *danseuses* of Toulouse-Lautrec's *Moulin Rouge*.

Loanna Haseltine is an American fashion designer living in Paris who specializes in handmade, artistic corsets. I met Loanna in her showroom in the Sentier garment district. Part showroom, part ladies boudoir—the corsets on display are

more like works of art than pieces of clothing. I needed to find out how a girl from Alaska found herself designing couture corsets in Paris.

**Haseltine**: Since I can remember, I was passionate about designing and making clothes. When I was twelve years old, I saw a program on haute couture with Karl Lagerfeld, where he described the process of couture in Paris. They talked about the Chambre Syndicale de la Haute Couture, which is THE school in Paris to learn couture. From the time I saw that show, it was my idea to come to Paris to learn couture and eventually open my own house.

I eventually did come to Paris for school. Once, while still at the Chambre Syndicale, I answered a pretty generic ad in *Le Figaro* that led to an (unpaid) internship for John Galliano! At the time he was completely unknown. There were five people in the workroom and five people in the studio. It was a very grassroots outfit. There, I worked as an assistant to Bruno Barbier who was the *chef d'atelier* and the main draper for the big presentation pieces that John would use for his shows. When Bruno left and went to Ocimar Versolato who was designing for Lanvin, I followed him and then followed him to Christian Lacroix after that.

I was still interning during all of this, and although I was learning a lot, I really needed to find a proper position. With Bruno's encouragement, I created a small collection and showed the photos of it in a book to different houses to try and find a paying job. My book eventually passed under the nose of the owner of Maria Luisa. At the time, it was the "Colette" of Paris fashion—if you were anybody, you had to be in Maria Luisa. I showed her my collection, she took some pieces for her store and things took off from there. Soon after, I started getting calls from the *Herald Tribune* and *W Magazine*. After that bit of publicity, buyers started contacting me and asking where they could see my collection. I started selling in lots of little boutiques around the world and before I knew it, I had a little business.

Tagged as "One to Watch" by *Women's Wear Daily*, soon Haseltine's pieces could be seen on the red carpet at Cannes as well as on *Sex and the City*'s Carrie Bradshaw on

television. Over the years, Haseltine has come to concentrate her business on the art of custom corsetry, which she sells through her Paris showroom and her online boutique.

**Parisian Party**: What's the difference between a custom corset, and a commercially made corset found even in a higher-end lingerie or specialty boutique?

**Haseltine**: The differences between a commercially made corset and a hand-crafted one are huge. The old saying "You get what you pay for" really applies in the case of a corset. Commercially made corsets are mass-produced garments created for looks only. A low-quality corset isn't designed or equipped for true waist shaping. They don't use a front stiffening busk, usually have cheap plastic and/or bendable boning, and factory standard stitching. So they don't hold their form and don't offer any support. But the biggest difference is that commercially manufactured corsets don't mold to the natural curves of your body like a handmade quality corset.

Our corsets are handmade completely in the traditional way by skilled corsetieres, who have specialized in authentic traditional corsetry. Many learned the craft from their parents and grandparents. Most of our pieces are one of a kind. We use quality fabric, luxury lining, and a canvas linen interlining to give comfort, good fit, and lasting durability. With each corset, I try to create a garment that's a work of art that will last to be passed down through generations.

**Parisian Party**: What are the inspirations for your designs?

**Haseltine**: My concept is that beauty comes from the juxtaposition of completely diverse elements. When you take two opposite colors on the color spectrum and you put them together, that's what creates strength and beauty. Oftentimes, I look for a conflict of elements that are very, very diverse or completely opposite and bring those things together. So I'll work with materials like silk chiffon and leather. I became quite a specialist in working in those two elements early on.

My pieces are also custom, so I work with clients on what appeals to them. That's the thing that I love about bridal clients; the piece is as much their dream as mine, so we create the piece together. I had a client who, since she was a little girl, always loved butterflies. But she's a sophisticated adult now, so underneath the lace on her corset we hid little quilted butterflies and then we embroidered her and her husband's names on the underneath of the other side. It's those small ways that you help realize someone else's dream.

**Parisian Party**: Who is the Haseltine client?

**Haseltine**: She's really diverse—I'm always amazed. I have clients who are musicians in rock bands who want to wear a custom corset on their album cover or for shows. I also have mothers whose daughters are getting married and want to wear a wedding corset, but want something flattering and unique. After the wedding, they'll pair the corset with a little jacket and a beautiful skirt; I've created pieces for celebrities who discovered my things in stores and then approached me to create a piece for them personally, as well. I once met Catherine Zeta Jones at a party while I was wearing one of my pieces. She loved it and then contacted me later to have a piece created for her.

**Parisian Party**: Tell me a bit about clients who aren't in Paris and would like to order online.

**Haseltine**: For the online store, I created a selection of thirty pieces. Clients can take their measurements and send them to us via the form on the site. Any of the corsets on the website can be used to create a custom piece as well. We can work with color or fabric. I have a technique to blow up images and print them directly on the fabric. I've created pieces with these beautiful, abstract images from nature. If a client has an image they'd like to use, I can work with them to incorporate it into the piece. The corsets are all made here in Paris and then shipped out worldwide direct. Here in Paris, the showroom is open by appointment only, where we're happy to receive clients and introduce them to Haseltine corsets.

Haseltine
67, rue Reaumur
75002 Paris, France
www.haseltine-paris.com

## French Wedding Tradition: The Normand Hole

You're at your very first French wedding reception and you can't believe that even though you sat down to eat well over two hours ago, they're *still* bringing out food, without a hint of an end in sight. Before you even made it to the table, you stuffed yourself full of *amuse-bouche* (appetizers): *Torsadées Feuilletées au Jambon, Tartinade de chèvre au basilic et à l'ail,* and some little round meat things that tasted like cheese. Once comfortably seated *à table* (at the table), you gorged yourself on slabs of *Foie Gras de Canard aux Figues* and *Son Chutney de Poire et Mangue,* then *Trois Crusacés pour Une Ecume* and *Son Coulis Pourpre* followed by an amazing *Magret de Canette Grillé Sauce Périgourdine.*

After the plates are cleared, you scan the room for the happy couple, certain that it's finally time to crack the croquembouche (the traditional French wedding cake made of crème-filled puff-pastry). Instead, a waiter appears in front of you and sets down a dainty glass of what looks like a scoop of ice cream but smells like fruity alcohol. Ah, the famous "hidden" French dinner course: *Le Trou Normand* (The Normand Hole).

Le Trou Normand is a strong alcohol served with a small scoop of sorbet that's served during French weddings and large dinners. The idea is to clean the palate and stimulate the appetite, to give you a feeling of emptiness so that you can go back and tuck more in. The tradition, which started in Normandy, goes back several centuries. Originally, it was just a small glass of apple brandy (Calvados) served midway between a big meal. These days, any number of alcohols and flavors of sorbet can be served, depending on the region of France that you're in or the course that is about to be served. Vodka and lemon sorbet go nicely with fish or seafood, whereas traditional Calvados and apple sorbet are perfect for foie gras.

To make your own Trou Normand, place one or two small scoops of high-quality sorbet (if you can't find apple sorbet in the store, feel free to substitute with lemon or lime) into a pretty martini glass or champagne coupe, then slowly pour the Calvados over it, top it off with a sprig of mint or lemon zest, *et voila!* It's a simple recipe that can easily be incorporated into any French or Paris-themed wedding celebration.

The idea is to *clean the palate* and stimulate the appetite, to give you a feeling of emptiness so that you can *go back* and stuff more in!

# Wedding Invitation Shopping in Paris

A person's stationery tells you almost as much about the individual as his or her shoes do. Is the person casual, funny, serious or just plain boring? Does the person walk the walk and talk the talk (letterpress text on 100 percent cotton 300 gm paper stock), or is she all talk and no action (generic laser print on 28-pound Hammermill)? Everyone knows the value of having good-quality, well-designed business cards. But what about social stationery and invitations? Getting a tepid invitation to a "fabulous" party is kind of like meeting a handsome French doctor and then noticing that he's wearing Birkenstocks and socks—the potential is there, but you're not exactly sure if you want to make the effort to see it through.

With this in mind, it's time to get thee to *la papeterie* (stationery shop)! First stop: Caractére in the 16th arrondissement—the Manolo of paper shops! From stunning couture invitations to luxurious Italian leather desk accessories, this store has it all. Maybe you want a classic look for the Sunday brunch that you're hosting, have note cards or invitations engraved with your monogram or select a motif from Caractére's huge catalog. If your style is more contemporary, you have the option of choosing a custom design from one of their exclusive graphic artists, like Veronique Deshayes.

*Le Must* (The Must) in Paris fine papers is Marie Papier in Montparnasse. If you're a paper-aholic like me, this is as close to "off the wagon" as you can get. Marie Papier is stocked from floor to ceiling with notebooks, albums, Japanese writing papers, single stationery sheets and envelopes in a whole host of colors and textures, announcement cards, pens, pencils, inks and gorgeous packets of note cards. In addition, Marie Papier offers a bespoke invitation service, with a multitude of papers and styles to choose from.

If you've got an itch to go completely DIY with your invitations, you must make a detour into l'Art du Papier. There are several of these stores around Paris as well as an online store. They carry rubber stamps, inks, boxed stationery sets and scrapbooking materials, as well as the full line of Artoz papers. If you're starved for inspiration, l'Art du Papier also hosts in-store classes and demonstrations.

While I appreciate the thought behind an e-invite just as much as the next girl, nothing beats the nostalgic jolt of excitement that I get when I see a hand-addressed invitation in my mailbox. Whether in Paris or Poughkeepsie, in my book, a gorgeous paper invitation equals a party that's not to be missed!

| CARACTÉRE | MARIE PAPIER | L'ART DU PAPIER |
|---|---|---|
| 4, rue Mesnil | 26, rue Vavin | 16, rue Daunou |
| 75016 Paris, France | 75006 Paris, France | 75002 Paris, France |
| www.caractere-france.com | www.marie-papier-paris.fr | www.art-du-papier.fr |

# Outfitting Your Parisian Bridal Trousseau

Ask any woman in the world where the most desirable lingerie comes from, and she'll undoubtedly say Paris. No "Fruit of the Loom Boy Briefs" to be found there. Lacy, sexy, beautiful women's undergarments are the staple in Paris.

Back in the day, a young woman and her mother would start collecting and sewing items for her trousseau years before she was even engaged! They stored the items in a heavy hand-carved wooden wardrobe or trunk, and when it was complete, the trousseau contained everything that the girl owned—everything that she needed to start her new married life. Trousseaus could contain quilts, china, silverware, pillows or linens, in addition to clothing and lingerie. In Victorian times, it was even à la mode to host a Trousseau Tea the day before a wedding, where the bride's family would invite people over and show off all the items in the girl's trousseau. Today's trousseau contains gorgeous lingerie, luxurious toiletries and fabulous going-away outfits, all packed into beautiful luggage.

# TROUSSEAU SHOPPING IN PARIS

If you'd like to go on your own Parisian trousseau shopping spree, your first stop HAS TO BE the glamorous boudoir of Chantal Thomass. This shop is a treasure-trove of intimate feminine goodies like bras, bustiers, stockings and dressing gowns as well as frou-frou accessories like pink lace-up umbrellas and black satin and lace handcuffs. Oh la la!

Another queen of the *intime* (intimate) is Fifi Chachnil. Since 1986, Fifi has been known for her gloriously feminine designs as well as her sense of humor and classic vintage style. Her lingerie is sold worldwide, but nothing beats a trip to one of her Parisian boutiques.

Those in the know, know where to find the most famous French lingerie—they visit Sabbia Rosa in the 6th arrondissement. This tiny shop lives up to the hype and is a favorite of fashionistas like Madonna, Naomi Campbell and Catherine Deneuve.

One other major element of the modern bridal trousseau is fragrance. For your Parisian trousseau, peek your head into one of the Annick Goutal boutiques and discover your new signature scent. Everything about these boutiques is feminine and flirty, and while you're there, treat yourself to one of their Boudoir Treatments for the Face or Body (or both!) If you want to try your hand at creating your own *lune de miel* (honeymoon) fragrance, sign up for an *Atelier du Parfumerie* at the world-renowned Guerlain boutique on the Champs-Elysées.

Once you have your trousseau together, you can't just toss it into any old Samsonite! You still have a wedding to pay for, so don't break the bank on *nouveau* Louis Vuitton, Hermès or Goyard. Instead, try scouting out Le Monde du Voyage in the Marche aux Puces at Saint-Ouen. This store has been specializing in vintage luggage for more than twenty years and will surely have the perfect *valise* (suitcase) to round out your Parisian bridal trousseau.

CHANTAL THOMASS
211, rue Saint-Honoré
75001 Paris, France
www.chantalthomass.fr

FIFI CHACHNIL
68, rue Jean-Jacques Rousseau
75001 Paris, France
www.fifichachnil.com/

SABBIA ROSA
73, rue Saints Pères
75006 Paris, France

GUERLAIN
68, Champs-Elysées
75008 Paris, France
www.guerlain.com

LE MONDE DU VOYAGE
Stand 15, Allée 3
108-110, rue des Rosiers
93400 Saint-Ouen, France
www.lemondeduvoyage.com

Today's trousseau contains *gorgeous lingerie,*

luxurious toiletries and fabulous going-away outfits,

all packed into *beautiful luggage.*

# Tête à Tête with Paris Wedding Photographer Ian Holmes

Ian Holmes is a dashing destination-wedding photographer based in Paris. Originally from the North of England, Ian came to Paris on a two-year contract to work for a pre-press firm and has ended up staying for more than a decade. He's sought after for his journalistic approach to wedding photography. His goal, he says, is to create images that tell the story of the day as it happened, not as the photographer directed it. Ian and I met in a café on the Boulevard Saint-Germaine one chilly morning this past spring to talk about wedding photography in Paris.

**Parisian Party:** How long have you been a wedding photographer in Paris?

**Holmes:** I actually "stumbled" into wedding photography whilst out in the States in 2008 when I was working as a photographer for a New York–based lifestyle magazine. My first-ever wedding was shot in Los Angeles. After that followed a brief spell in England before returning to Paris.

**Parisian Party:** What advice do you have for couples choosing a wedding photographer from a distance?

**Holmes:** The majority of clients choosing a wedding photographer overseas browse websites to find something aesthetically pleasing, a style that catches their eye. However, it's important to look beyond a photographer's portfolio, which comprises a handful of their very best shots. Take some time browsing the photographer's blog; it should give more of an idea of how they approach a wedding from beginning to end. It can (or should) also give an insight into the photographer's personality. How pro-active are they in answering emails or any questions or concerns? Are they open to a conference call or Skype meeting? While the photos are obviously of primary concern, it's important to look beyond that. Your wedding photographer is going to be a huge part of your day and it's important that he or she is someone you'll feel comfortable being around. If they have the best portfolio in the world but you feel you don't really click with the person, my advice would be to move on to someone else.

**Parisian Party:** I know that many clients want a photo session around Paris at some point during their wedding. What advice do you have for couples planning this sort of session?

**Holmes:** One of my favorite parts of a Paris-based wedding is actually a photo shoot around the city. For someone not familiar with Paris, a great starting point for location scouting would be to browse the Internet (probably beginning with the photographer's website), highlighting areas that appeal to them. If you then begin discussing the shoot with the photographer, he or she should be able to put together an itinerary based on the client's timescale, mode of transport and desired locations. Regarding what to wear, a wedding gown always looks stunning on the city streets; however, less formal outfits may give more variation to the images as well as keeping the wedding gown pristine for the ceremony. Another consideration is whether to have the shoot before or after the ceremony. The advantage of the shoot before the ceremony is that the couple can enjoy their time with guests afterwards. The disadvantage (if the gown is worn) is the probability of a slightly dirty dress. For a wedding shoot I always recommend a chauffeur-driven car to take us around the city. Not only is it practical, allowing us to take in more locations, a beautiful, classic car makes a great addition to the photos.

**Parisian Party:** What are your top "money shot" locations for couples that hire you for a Paris wedding photo shoot?

**Holmes:** I always enjoy showing off the more subtle side of Paris in my photos. I've found it's often the hidden areas that clients enjoy discovering the most—the old passages, a Paris backstreet, etc. Of course most clients want some recognizable landmarks included. I try to get a nice balance of the two.

**Parisian Party:** You have clients from all over the world who come to Paris for either wedding or engagement photos, but you also have a very strong Paris-based clientele. What are some of the differences between these clients? What do Parisian wedding couples look for in their photo shoots?

**Holmes**: With destination clients, a big part of their photography is showing off the city. The majority wants some of the classic Paris landmarks in the photos, the Eiffel Tower, the Louvre, one of the famous bridges, etc. I try and incorporate the landmarks with some of the hidden sides of the city to add a little variation. Clients often get back to me and let me know which images they had printed to hang on their walls, and generally it's one of the images featuring an iconic Parisian landmark.

Parisians, on the other hand, aren't particularly bothered about the Eiffel Tower. Most of them catch sight of it every day on their way to and from work. They often want to feature their local neighborhood. For example, I once had a couple that lived on a very lively pedestrian shopping street. This street had bakers, butchers, fruit shops, patisseries, wine stores—everything. They basically did their grocery shopping on their wedding day in full wedding attire. It was a fun shoot that turned a lot of heads.

**Parisian Party**: I know this may be a silly question, but why do you choose to be a wedding photographer in Paris?

**Holmes**: Paris has to be one of the world's most stunning locations for a destination wedding. Seeing the city through my client's eyes keeps it feeling fresh and exciting. The fact that I have such a magnificent backdrop to my images, get to work with some amazing people whilst doing a job I love makes me feel extremely fortunate.

Ian Holmes, Photographer
www.ianholmes.net
Tel: +33 (0) 6 73 73 38 49

# PAMELA & MATT

Inspired by their mutual love of the modern classic French film *Amélie Poulain*,
Pamela and Matt's sweet, intimate wedding celebrated both the beauty and offbeat
charm of Montmartre as well as the movie. Like in the film, red was a predominant
color throughout their event—in the vintage French car they rented to zip around
town, in the Moulin Rouge, which was one of the landmark backdrops for their
pre-ceremony photo session, and in the macarons and raspberries (Amélie's favorite fruit) that were served during their picnic reception on the banks of the Seine.

WEDDING DESIGN AND COORDINATION
Kim Petyt
Parisian Events
www.parisianevents.com

PHOTOGRAPHY
Milos and Natasa Horvat
www.miloshorvat.com

DRESS
Thirteen by Rivini
www.rivini.com

HAIR AND MAKEUP
James
www.jmsbyjames.come

HAIR FASCINATOR
Jennifer Leigh Veils
www.jenniferleighveils.com

EARRINGS AND WEDDING BANDS
Ramiro Ortego
www.finessejewelers.net

WAISTCOAT
Calvin Klein

BOWTIE
Xoelle
www.etsy.com/shop/xoelle

CATERER
Kent Party Solutions
www.kentpartysolutions.com

# Parisian Chic

- ⚜ PARISIAN COLOR PALETTE: Pure white, brushed aluminum, neutral gray and aurora yellow

IMAGINE A *PORTE OUVERTE* (GALLERY WALK) IN SAINT-GERMAINE-DES-PRÈS. PARISIAN CHIC IS FASHIONABLE, URBAN, STREAMLINED, CLEAN, HIP AND FRESH, WITH THE FLAIR OF A MODERN PARISIAN GALLERY, WHERE ART AND ROMANCE MEET, ETERNALLY ENTANGLED IN THE HEART OF THE "BON CHIC BON GENRE" OF PARIS.

DESIGN AND STYLING
Kim Petyt, Parisian Events
www.parisianevents.com

VENUE
Private loft

PHOTOGRAPHY
Ian Holmes
www.ianholmes.net

INVITATIONS
Paper + Cup
www.papercupdesign.com

FAVORS
La Citronade Citron-Menthe
Eau de Source
Jérôme Biarritz
www.jeromebiarritz.blogspot.fr

CAKE
Sugarplum Cake Shop
www.sugarplumcakeshop.com

VINTAGE BROOCH
Au Grenier de Lucie
www.augrenierdelucie.com

## Tête à Tête with Paris Wedding Dress Designer Reinaldo Alvarez

I fell in love with Reinaldo Alvarez' designs at the very first Parisian wedding salon, Salon de Mariage, that I went to more than ten years ago. Amidst all the fluff, feathers and girlie frou-frou that many of the French bridal designers were catering to at the time, here was a collection that was chic, sophisticated and elegant—clearly designed for a *woman*. I had an opportunity to meet him not too long after that first show and was completely smitten with his sense of humor and Latin charm. I've been stalking him ever since.

Reinaldo Alvarez was born in Bayamon, Puerto Rico. He studied fashion design at Parsons School of Design and FIT in New York, and worked extensively on 7th Avenue (including designing accessories for Oscar de la Renta) before taking the leap and moving to Paris. He opened his atelier in the Marais more than ten years ago. We met in his showroom in the Marais, which, like his designs, is chic, sleek and devoid of any unnecessary fussiness. After a quick coffee and a bit of "off-the-record" gossip, we got down to the business at hand.

**Parisian Party**: Describe the Reinaldo Alvarez style.

**Alvarez**: A client once defined my dresses as "the definitive fusion between elegance and simplicity," and I think that's true. I like to say that my designs are timeless. For me, it's important that a bride doesn't look at her wedding photos in twenty years, and think that she looks "outdated."

**Parisian Party**: Who do you design for?

**Alvarez**: The Reinaldo Alvarez client is the BCBG Parisienne who is *allergique* to lace, rhinestones, beads, tulle and feathers. She wants a beautiful dress in a beautiful fabric that is as simple as possible. I love working in silk dupioni, silk gazar, organza jacquard . . . elegant fabrics that are easy to sculpt.

**Parisian Party**: In addition to your wedding gowns, you also have a strong collection of cocktail and evening wear. Can you tell more about that?

**Alvarez:** It's a very contemporary collection, comprised of elegant and practical pieces that go from day to night with a simple change of accessories. It has unique textures and embroidery as decoration. Skirts, pants and jackets are combined with very large, very modern silhouettes. These are simple, elegant looks for cocktail, mother of the bride or even civil wedding ceremonies.

**Parisian Party:** I think a lot of them could even work for bridesmaid dresses . . .

**Alvarez:** Yes, for the British or American brides for their *témoins* (witnesses).

**Parisian Party:** What is the process for ordering a Reinaldo Alvarez piece?

**Alvarez:** Our dresses are made to order and typically take three fittings. We work with a client to give her the dress she wants. If she wants this style, in this fabric, with this length . . . she can change whatever she likes.

**Parisian Party:** And how long does it take to receive the final piece?

**Alvarez:** From start to finish, around six or seven months.

**Parisian Party:** Finally, who is your Parisian style icon? Who do you think defines the Parisian woman?

**Alvarez:** That's simple—for me, it's Anna Mouglalis. No explanation needed!

At the forefront of couture wedding design for some time now in Paris, if you're a stylish American bride looking for a uniquely Parisian look for your wedding day, your answer is Reinaldo Alvarez.

REINALDO ALVAREZ
9, rue Jarente
75004 Paris, France
www.reinaldo-alvarez.com

## LE MUR DES JE T'AIME:
## THE WALL OF I LOVE YOUS

In the Square Jehan-Rictus, just behind the Abbesses metro station in the 18th arrondissement, stands a sweet tribute to one of the most powerful phrases in the world. Back in 1992, French musician Frédéric Baron began collecting "I love yous," asking neighbors, friends and strangers all around Paris to write "I love you" in their own language on little pieces of paper. When he was finished, he had collected 1,000 I Love Yous in more than 300 languages, which he and artist/calligrapher Claire Kito then translated onto glazed tiles to create the wall.

The artist writes on his website: "To go among others and ask them to write 'I love you' is to create a passport which erases borders and opens hearts. I took note of it, but I understood at the same time, that it was not only a question of words and that love is subject to other laws. Cocteau said, 'There is no love, there is only proof of love.' One does not play with love. It is a serious affair. Even without knowing what I wanted to do with them, the 'I love yous' took me a long way. They forced me to treat them like a real job. Please understand, I certainly do not pretend to have accomplished a scientific work. On the contrary, if this venture has succeeded it's because it has conserved its romantic side, its original purity. Men and women of all races and all walks of life have left their trace on paper like a gift fallen from heaven. A free gesture."

Why not create your own *mur des je t'aime* at your Paris-themed wedding by covering a designated wall with craft paper and encouraging guests to leave their own *mots doux* (sweet nothings) with paint pens and markers. Once the ink has dried, use the wall as a backdrop for a Paris-inspired DIY photo booth!

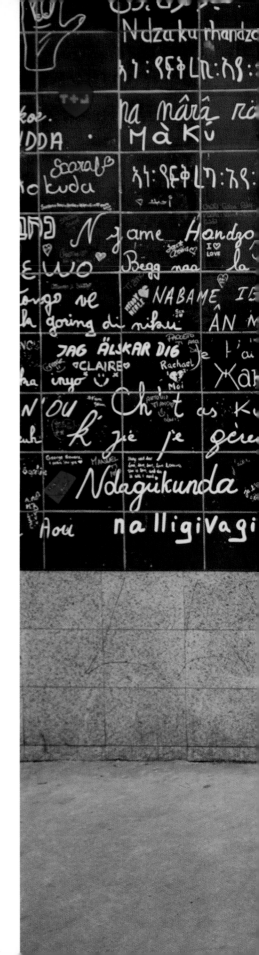

Nalingi yo
SZERETLEK
mye nTondo
NIMITZTLAZÒTLA
ASSAVAKKIT
KIYAHURATA
EREHMEH
ALOR
KICINYOH
I LOVE YOU
NAN WE
ADAM + GREG
N DAKUYANDA

# American Wedding Cakes in Paris: Sugarplum Cake Shop

Ask any expat anywhere in the world and they'll tell you that no matter how much you love your adopted country, every once in a while, you need a little bit of home. My home away from home in Paris is Sugarplum Cake Shop. Created by three North American expats who've found their calling in bringing classic American pastries to Paris, Sugarplum Cake Shop, in the historical 5th arrondissement, serves up classics like carrot cake, cheesecake and apple pie alongside a fabulous selection of organic teas and coffees. Everything is baked on-site using the freshest local ingredients. Sugarplum Cake Shop has also almost single-handedly created the current French craze for American-style wedding cakes. Their fondant and butter cream creations are at the top of the must-have list for today's trendy Parisian brides. While chugging down slabs of carrot cake and lattés one day, I asked the Sugarplums if having the coffee shop alongside the cake business affected their introduction into the Parisian wedding scene.

**Sugarplum:** Having the boutique open has been a really valuable vehicle for introducing American-style cakes to France. Through the boutique, we've been able to present the different cake flavors and combinations and pinpoint those most likely to please both our French and American clientele. Once, while we were under construction in 2010, Krista was using our boutique to cover models for a wedding fair. As she was kneading a mountain of blue fondant, a dapper French gentleman popped his head inside and asked what kind of bread is made from blue dough. When she told him she was making a cake, he looked blankly at her for a moment and then said, *"Bon courage,"* in a dubious tone. We've become a neighborhood landmark since then, and our coffee shop is filled with Parisians young and old. It's wonderful walking through the boutique and seeing an enthusiastic child covered in cupcake frosting, while next to him, his elegant *grandmère* (grandmother) cuts her Rice Krispie square with a knife and fork.

**Parisian Party:** So, why did you create Sugarplum Cake shop? With all of its amazing patisseries, what did you think Paris was missing?

**Sugarplum:** Well, one of the first reasons we wanted to open Sugarplum was about making real American pastries, the way we were taught by our mamas and aunties and grandmas. We wanted to make cakes with real ingredients and not from box mixes, just flour, eggs, sugar, milk and chocolate . . . We're incredibly lucky to be able to work with some of the very best quality ingredients our planet has to offer. Have you ever tasted *beurre de Normandy* (Normandy butter)? There is nothing better. Anywhere. When we opened our coffee shop, we hoped to create a place where people like us felt comfy and at home. France is a wonderful place to live, so much so that I've been here

for eighteen years, but every once in a while it's nice to have some back-home cozy and charm.

It's funny, because when we first opened, our French clients were more inclined to stick to traditional "French" flavors such as rose, almond, violet and pistachio. As our reputation grows, however, our French clients are starting to be more adventurous, choosing American flavors like peanut butter, mint chocolate and Oreo.

**Parisian Party:** What are ways that you've incorporated French and American touches into a cake design, for bi-cultural weddings, for instance?

*Sugarplum Cake Shop* has almost single-handedly spearheaded the *current French craze* for American-style wedding cakes.

**Sugarplum**: One of our most popular cake designs combines a stacked cake in a soft pastel color, ringed with French macarons and tied up with silk ribbons. Tall, slender cakes mimic the shape of the traditional French wedding dessert, the croquembouche, and are a popular choice for couples that wish to incorporate both desserts into their menu.

**Parisian Party**: What do you see as the current trends in wedding cakes in Paris? Is the stacked American-style cake a fad in France, or do you think it's becoming more commonplace?

**Sugarplum**: Wedding cake trends closely follow the styles and palettes of fashion trends. In Paris, one can be inspired by merely sitting in our coffee shop and watching the beautiful people walk by. In cake couture, smaller, more intricately decorated cakes are stealing the stage as well as color-blocked cakes and lace details. Also, French couples are currently showing a fascination with New York. We've done almost a dozen NYC-themed wedding cakes. While these fresh styles are breathing new life into cake culture, the traditional white wedding cake is still a timeless classic.

I don't think that American-style cakes are a fad in Paris. Of course, they'll never replace the wonderful French pastry traditions, but I believe that Paris will continue to embrace the wedding cake as a beautiful addition to their tables.

Sugarplum Cake Shop
68, rue du Cardinal Lemoine
75005 Paris, France
www.sugarplumcakeshop.com

# Party on the Seine:
# A Visit with Yachts de Paris

As anyone who has spent time online looking for a dinner cruise in Paris can tell you, there are A LOT of options out there. Google "dinner on the Seine" and you'll be treated to pages and pages of companies offering romantic, enchanting and unforgettable evenings on the river Seine. But if you're 3,000 miles away, how can you tell one from the other? For obvious reasons, my first advice would be to hire a professional, like a wedding planner in Paris to help you, but my SECOND piece of advice would be to look to Yachts de Paris. In my opinion, Yachts de Paris offers the finest dining experience on water in Paris. They offer a luxe fleet with an impressive menu and impeccable service. I had the opportunity to sit down with the director of commercial operations of Yachts de Paris, and she filled me in on just what makes Yachts de Paris so special.

**Parisian Party**: Let's start with a little background information. How many boats are there in the Yachts de Paris fleet?

**Yachts de Paris**: We have a range of eight boats, starting with the smallest, *Cachemire,* which can host up to twelve guests maximum, right up to *Paquebot,* which can accommodate up to 400 guests.

**Parisian Party**: One of the things that I love about working with Yachts de Paris is that each boat has its own style. How do you go about matching a yacht with a client? Do you look at their own individual style, or is it just based on the size of their party?

**Yachts de Paris**: We look at both really. If it's a wedding proposal, for instance, it makes sense to do it on *Cachmire* since it's our most intimate boat. For a small, sit-down reception, say up to fifty guests, clients would have a choice between *Acajou* and *Victoria,* which have the same capacity but different styles. *Acajou* is very classic, with a lot of light wooden features, and would be more for a traditional client looking to host a more traditional affair, whereas *Victoria* is decorated in deep reds, browns and brushed aluminum touches, which would definitely suit clients with more neo-classical tastes.

**Parisian Party:** Speaking of decoration, another thing that is special about working with Yachts de Paris is the choice of ambiances that are available to choose from.

**Yachts de Paris:** Yes, we worked with a designer to give each boat its own individual style. Each boat has a standard offering. For some boats, it's a crisp classical look, with white china, white linens, very classic. Other boats may have a more modern look with gray or black tableware and linens. From those standard offerings, clients can modify and choose from anything else that we offer. They may want to change the shape of their stemware or color of linens, for example. Working with clients or their wedding designer, we can create an individual, customized look just for their event.

**Parisian Party:** Typically, when I first start working with destination clients, I find that they know they want to get married in Paris, but they don't really know if they

want to get married on the Seine, in a chateau, in a hotel or what. What would you say are some benefits of hosting a destination event in Paris on the water?

**Yachts de Paris:** Well, if you're comparing getting married on the Seine with a venue like a hotel or other reception site, the biggest benefit of course is the location. You're actually moving through the heart and history of Paris. It's hard to compare other things with that!

**Parisian Party:** So true! But there are so many cruise options in Paris. If you're trying to plan a wedding from overseas, it really can be hard to compare, especially since they all seem to be offering the same thing. What do you think sets Yachts de Paris apart from some of the other cruise companies in Paris?

**Yachts de Paris:** Speaking honestly, we are the best (laughs)! You're right, though. There are a lot of companies on the river, and people do have to be careful. Some

In my *opinion,* Yachts de Paris offers the *finest dining experience* on water in Paris.

of them are private owners who stopped using the boat for commercial use, like transporting rice and stuff, and then rebuilt the boat for a restaurant. They have absolutely no experience. This is actually very dangerous for someone who is trying to book on his or her own instead of with a wedding planner or agency. They see that a certain boat is cheaper than others, and they'll make their decision based on that. Those are, of course, extreme situations. You also have companies like Bateaux Parisian, for instance, which are experienced and professional and offer more standardized services. For a certain price, you are offered a certain package and you must take that package. You can't redecorate with that sort of fleet, for instance. There's not much room for customization. Also, with some of these other companies, you must have a minimum number of guests before you can privatize a boat, otherwise you must share the boat with other parties. Because our fleet is so varied, we're able to offer privatization with as little as two guests!

Another major factor that sets us apart is our extraordinary know-how in our service, staff and food. We work with Lenôtre, one of the most well-known caterers in Paris. Our clients trust us and feel comfortable with us because they know that we know how to do it. The boats are amazing. They are very well taken care of, and our service is impeccable. In all honesty, we don't see other cruise companies as our competition, we consider ourselves to be in the same league as other fine dining establishments, like service that you'd find at the George V.

YACHTS DE PARIS
Port Henri IV
75004 Paris, France
www.entreprises.yachtsdeparis.fr

# Planning Your Parisian Wedding Dress Shopping Trip

If you're thinking about a quick little trip to Paris to shop for your wedding dress, you may be in for a big surprise. While malls and Main Streets across America are teaming with one-stop bridal emporiums like Kleinfelds and David's Bridal, most bridal boutiques in Paris only carry one designer or label. So if you've narrowed your wish-list down to, say, Delphine Manivet, Meryl Suissa, Max Chaoul and Suzanne Ermann, with the idea to check out a few others along the way, be prepared to visit four *different* ateliers, with each visit lasting a minimum of one and a half hours (if you're visiting on a weekend and planning to try dresses on). With most boutiques closed on Sundays, your "weekend" buying trip in Paris could end up with you only seeing a handful of dresses and a whole lot of frustration.

If you want to maximize your time during your Paris wedding dress buying trip, I suggest hitting up the major department stores first—Printemps, Galeries Lafayette and Le Bon Marché all have bridal levels offering a small selection of a number of labels. Paris has several Pronovias, Pronuptia and Rosa Clara boutiques as well, but their collections may be what you would find at your home locations. The gold mine of wedding dress options in Paris is Metal Flaque. Since 2009, Metal Flaque has been the main source in France to find designers like Vera Wang, Monique Lhuillier, Jenny Packham, Marchesa and more.

Whether you choose to go the exclusive boutique route, or prefer to power through the multi-label options, keep in mind that for many Parisian bridal stores, walk-ins can be frowned upon. And if you plan to try on dresses, a rendezvous (appointment) should be made in advance.

DELPHINE MANIVET
93, rue du faubourg Saint-Honoré
75008 Paris, France
www.delphinemanivet.com

MAX CHAOUL
55, quai des Grands Augustins
75006 Paris, France
www.maxchaoulcouture.com

SUZANNE ERMANN
130, rue de Turenne
75003 Paris, France
www.suzanne-ermann.com

MERYL SUISSA
15, rue de Surène
75008 Paris, France
www.merylsuissa.com

PRINTEMPS MARIAGE
64, boulevard Haussmann
75009 Paris, France
www.listes-mariage.printemps.com

GALERIES LAFAYETTE HAUSSMANN
40, boulevard Haussmann
75009 Paris, France
www.galerieslafayette.com

LE BON MARCHE
24, rue de Sèvres
75007 Paris, France
www.mariage.lebonmarche.fr

METAL FLAQUE
9, rue de l'Échelle
75001 Paris, France
www.metalflaque.fr

For many *bridal vendors* in Paris, walk-ins can be frowned upon. And if you plan *to try dresses on,* a *rendezvous* (appointment) must be made in advance.

# Modern Bachelor Night in Paris

I received an email the other day from a groom-to-be in the United States who was frustrated because he couldn't find information online about spa treatments for men in Paris. He and his Merry Band of Metrosexuals are foregoing the stereotypical Stag Night in Paris in Pigalle and have chosen instead to spend the day before his Parisian wedding getting primped and pampered. His future bride is understandably ecstatic. Having had the pleasure of witnessing those mobs of drunken bachelors firsthand when I lived near Pigalle in my former life, I really appreciate Groom-to-Be's discretion. So here you go, boys. I'm just happy to help.

- ⚜ The Four Seasons Hotel: The spa in the Four Seasons George V features a full menu of treatments for men, including the "It's a Man's World," which includes a green tea refresher, facial, herbal deep cleansing back treatment, Swedish massage and a classic manicure or pedicure, served with green tea.

- ⚜ Institut Marc Delacre: Located on Avenue George V, this was the first institute for hair and beauty treatment in Paris that was conceived entirely for men.

- ⚜ Nickel: You'll find "Serious Skin Care for Men" at this trendy man's spa and salon in the Marais.

- ⚜ Il Fait Beau: Also located in the Marais, Il Fait Beau offers massages, laser hair removal, manicures, pedicures and teeth whitening to help keep beautiful men looking their best.

- ⚜ Alain, Maitre Barbier: This is an old-fashioned Parisian barbershop (and museum) where you'll be treated to a *rasoir à l'ancienne* with a sharpened straight razor and hot towel treatment. Alain also gives private lessons in the art of shaving.

THE FOUR SEASONS HOTEL
35, avenue George V
75008 Paris, France
www.fourseasons.com/paris/

INSTITUT MARC DELACRE
17, avenue George V
75008 Paris, France
www.cercledelacre.com/fr

NICKEL
48, rue de Francs Bourgeois
75003 Paris, France
www.nickel.fr

IL FAIT BEAU
51, rue des Archives
75003 Paris, France
www.institut-beaute75.fr

ALAIN, MAITRE BARBIER
8, rue Saint-Claude
75003 Paris, France
www.maitrebarbier.com

## Tête à Tête with Parisian Wedding Shoe Designer Vouelle

You've got the dress, earrings, ring, tickets to Paris, and something old, new, borrowed, etc. But we ALL know the look will never be complete without the perfect shoes. That's the predicament that Californian Melissa Regan de Vogele found herself in right before her Paris wedding when she still hadn't found her dream shoes. That experience led her to create Vouelle, a Paris-based wedding and cocktail shoe company, in 2008. Since then, Vouelle has quickly become one of the top stops on the Parisian bride's "must have" list. I met up with Melissa in her cozy, *typiquement* (typical) Parisian showroom to speak with her about the Vouelle bridal collection.

**Parisian Party**: You were living in Paris when you got engaged, which is pretty much every American girl's dream as far as shopping for her wedding outfit goes. But your experience actually led you to create your company, didn't it?

**Melissa de Vogele**: Yes, I was living in Paris but am from the Bay Area and was organizing my wedding there. I had found my dress here in Paris but was having trouble finding shoes. I ended up buying a pair that was esthetically beautiful but incredibly uncomfortable. They cost a fortune, but by the end of the night, I couldn't walk anymore! That experience led me to approach designer Michelle Boor, who was a really good friend of mine, about launching a collection of bridal shoes here. And it grew from there!

**Parisian Party**: Who is the Vouelle bridal client?

**Melissa de Vogele**: We tend to see two types of French bride: We see the very classic, seiziéme (16th arrondissement, weathly, conservative, preppy) bride. She will typically go for a traditional *escarpin* (pump), something very time-honored, very prim and proper. Our other French bride is very fashionable and tapped into the Paris scene. She has read about us and wants a shoe that none of her

group has seen before, something very different. The brides that contact us from the U.S. really want something that's European, they want the sophistication and to have something that can't be found everywhere else. Our shoes make the American bride feel really special. Here in the showroom, besides local clients, we receive a lot of U.K. brides and a lot of Swiss. We also get a lot of referrals from local dress designers. We work quite closely with Max Chaoul, for instance, Ana Quasoar, Suzanne Ehrmann, and collaborate off and on with other Parisian-based designers.

**Parisian Party**: What can a bride expect on a visit to Vouelle?

**Melissa de Vogele**: We receive clients here in our showroom by rendezvous. We encourage them to come with a swatch or a photo of their dress, and then we take it from there. We have what we call our "show stoppers," like the Dana, which is usually what brings a bride in to us, but one of our best sellers is actually a basic escarpin on a medium-height heel. It's a sophisticated, stylish design that gives comfort. We're able to do customization as well, so starting with the basic escarpin, we can build from there. We can add dentelle from the bride's dress, for instance, we can add on Swarovski crystals or other treatments that directly match her dress.

**Parisian Party**: Tell me a bit about the Vouelle bridal collection.

**Melissa de Vogele**: We have a bridal collection of about ten styles that are really what "our" brides want. We've recently started using platforms for the first time. We also love these little satin thongs with handmade organza fans. We have a lot of brides who are married in Saint-Tropez and they want something that's a bit more suitable. We'll always keep the classic base, but we like to add more styles that are a bit less traditional.

One trend that we're seeing overall is that brides are breaking away from tradition. In the past, there were set rules—"Never show your toes," etc. Today's bride asks if she HAS to wear a certain shoe, when what she WANTS is much more forward, more modern. Our Gina, for instance, with the transparent plastic panels, has done really well. It's an haute couture shoe that is very untraditional. So, I think that the trend is that there are no more rules. Today's brides are breaking the mold.

**Parisian Party**: How can fashionable brides outside of Europe shop Vouelle?

**Melissa de Vogele**: Our e-commerce site is integrated into our website, which means brides are able to shop Vouelle from around the world.

Vouelle
167, boulevard Haussemann
75008 Paris, France
www.vouelle.com

*Daring.*

Discriminating.

*Stylish.* Offbeat.

Above all else, the

couple that chooses

to get married in

Paris is *unique.*

Vintage chic weddings have taken the world by storm, and Paris is no different. Lindsay and Josh's Parisian wedding was inspired by 1950s Bourjois Cosmetics magazine ads and images of vintage debutante balls at the Hotel Crillon. Their discerning tastes mixed with their youthful energy helped make their chic Parisian celebration modern, sophisticated and fun.

WEDDING DESIGN AND COORDINATION
Kim Petyt, Parisian Events
www.parisianevents.com

PHOTOGRAPHY
Ian Holmes
www.ianholmes.net

VENUE
Maison des Polytechniciens

FLOWERS
Atelier Lieu-Dit
www.lieu-dit-paris.fr

CAKE
Sugarplum Cake Shop
www.sugarplumcakeshop.com

DRESS
Modeca be Enzoani
www.enzoani.com

SHOES
Badgley Mischka
www.badgleymischka.com

SUIT
Tommy Hilfiger

MENU AND PLACECARDS
Hello Lucky Stationery
www.hellolucky.com

BOUTONNIERE
One Happy Girl
www.etsy.com/shop/onehappygirl

# Montparnasse Magnifique: The 1920s Parisian Wedding

❧ PARISIAN COLOR PALETTE: Golden ochre, pale gray, pure white floating on clear crystal with the slightest touch of peacock blue

THE 1920S PARISIAN WEDDING: ART DÉCO, ELEGANT, REFINED YET JAZZY; SCOTT AND ZELDA IN *LES ANNÉES FOLLES;* MODERN SOPHISTICATION WITH A SUBTLE HINT OF RETRO CHARM.

DESIGN AND STYLING
Kim Petyt, Parisian Events
www.parisianevents.com

PHOTOGRAPHY
Ian Holmes, www.ianholmes.net

CAKE
Sugarplum Cake Shop
www.sugarplumcakeshop.com

FLOWERS
Atelier Lieu-Dit
www.lieu-dit-paris.fr

MENU
Paper + Cup
www.papercupdesign.com

VENUE
Dany Art Deco, Marche Aux Puces
Saint-Ouen, Paris, www.bdvdeco.com

## Tête à Tête with Haute Couturier Fanny Liautard

Meeting Fanny Liautard is like meeting a grande dame from another era. The way she gestures when she speaks, the way she sweeps through her atelier and the way she enchants you with the stories of her life. Her authenticity and commitment to her vision is so strong, you feel yourself being swept up and taken back in time as you listen to her talk. She told me about her beginnings in haute couture and the process and inspirations for her designs.

**Fanny Liautard:** Growing up, I knew I was an artist at heart. I wrote and drew and just created. So the question for me was would I be a writer, a sculptor, a painter. I would *create*, I just didn't know which direction I would go in. Then I discovered fashion. I realized that haute couture was art—art that you can live in! If I created haute couture, I would be able to live and move in my art. It was the most complete sensation, a way to fully experience my art. That's how I chose fashion and haute couture

as my way of life. I studied fashion at the Ecole de la Chambre Syndicale de la Haute Couture. After studying fashion, I worked with Hubert de Givenchy to learn the trade. That's where I learned to be precise and to perfect my skills.

**Parisian Party**: Your dresses have a rare, timeless quality to them. They cross many eras but are modern and fashion-forward at the same time. Where do you get your inspirations?

**Fanny Liautard**: The ideas behind my pieces come from many different places, sometimes in something that I hear or a film that I see. I extend that story and create a gown that often has nothing to do with the original subject. For example, I often "dress" Grace Kelly and Greta Garbo. I re-create costumes for them inspired by their appearance, their elegance, their movements. Sometimes I pay tributes to other designers—Christian Dior, Paul Poiret, Chanel. I re-create a garment by taking, for example, an idea, an item, and reworking it my way. Re-create it with my visions. It could be a flower, a seam, a cutting. I created a fold called the "Dior fold." I have a neckline inspired by a Paul Poiret or a 1930s Coco Chanel dress. This is the spirit in which I create. I re-imagine, rework, reinterpret. But these are all starting points. The first sketch of a dress will start like that, and then the second version will elaborate on it or go off in another direction. But this is how I typically start.

**Parisian Party**: Is there a typical Fanny Liautard client?

**Fanny Liautard**: I don't really have a typical client. I think what the women who I dress have in common is that they are cultivated and appreciate beauty and aesthetics. There's no particular age to my clients. Last year, for example, I had several clients who were very young—fourteen and eighteen years old. I made their gowns for their first dances. I have no limit. My client has no age. They are just cultivated. My clients could order a gown for a first ball just as well as for a second or third marriage. My bridal clients are independent women who aren't too traditional. They decide for themselves and don't expect their mothers to decide for them. What brings us all together is this affinity of art deco, a vision of fashion, a way of life. So, yes, that's the link.

**Parisian Party:** How much customization do you do? How far are you willing to veer from your original vision? Do you do every change a client asks for?

**Fanny Liautard:** (Laughing) Well, I do if I like it. There's just one condition: I must be convinced that a change is necessary. I must first be satisfied because I project myself on my creations. The gown carries my name. So, I must be convinced before I make certain design modifications. Otherwise, it's just not possible.

**Parisian Party:** Your designs are heavily influenced by the 1920s and 1930s, which is an era that we Americans are just fascinated with. What do you think is so appealing about this time in Paris?

**Fanny Liautard:** Artists concentrated on Paris during this time. It was the center of everything—everything! Paris was the center of the creative world. At the same time, there was the German Bauhaus, there was Jean-Michel Frank and the wonderful people in New York. But perhaps the greatest movement was in Paris. It was the center of art, music, ballet. Even the Ballets Russes came to Paris. Nijinksi and everything. Yes, everyone's dream was to be in Paris during that time. It was the place where everyone found himself, even Americans. I think

my designs embody this era. I think my gowns are sensual, free, unrestricted, right and graceful—like *les années folles* (crazy years) in Paris. This is my way of being and the way I see life. This is my style, that's all.

Fanny Liautard
13, rue Saint-Florentin
75008 Paris, France
www.fannyliautard.com

"I think my gowns are *sensual,* free, *unrestricted,* right and *graceful.*"

# Vintage Jewelry Shopping at the Paris Flea Market

Founded in 1987 by Franco-British couple Lucie Ellis and Alain Dufour, Au Grenier de Lucie in the Marché Aux Puces in Paris has been on the "must see" lists for vintage jewelry lovers from around the globe for nearly a quarter of a century. Since her retirement in 2005, Lucie's son and daughter-in-law, Jason and Heidi Ellis, have continued her passion for vintage fashion, growing the business so much that in 2009 they moved into a larger space in the Puces, at the Marché Vernaison.

Au Grenier de Lucie offers a whole range of costume jewelry dating from the 1920s to the present. Their jewelry is sourced worldwide and includes pieces from French designers such as Chanel, Yves St. Laurent, Lanvin, Lacroix and American classics like Miriam Haskell and Joseff of Hollywood.

During Paris Fashion Week, their sweet little shop is bursting at the seams with fashion editors from *Vogue, Elle* and *Harper's Bazaar*—all looking for that unique piece. They pride themselves on the fact that they can guarantee a special something for everyone, even a princess. They also carry a range of rare nineteenth-century crowns that they've collected from churches around France.

They pride themselves on the fact that they can guarantee a *special something* for everyone, even a *princess.*

Heidi and Jason took me exploring through their precious treasure-trove, and spoke to me about what native Parisians are on the hunt for when looking for vintage *bijoux fantasie* (costume jewelry).

**Heidi Ellis:** The typical French client always knows what she's looking for and what suits her best. She's not driven by designer names but by her desire to get it right. Many Parisian women opt for the classic pearls and simple designs. As regard to French designers, they appear to be particularly drawn towards Christian Dior 1960s pieces. However, the younger Parisian girls love Balenciaga and Lanvin. Parisian women also opt for Miriam Haskell 1940s to 50s pieces, as they do Bijoux Heart one-of-a-kind pieces. Chanel has long been a favorite for all women everywhere, of course, and her stunning pieces are always sought after. Other highly regarded designers include Yves St. Laurent and more recently Christian Lacroix. However, for some it is not about the designer but about which piece draws them in, lights up their faces and makes them feel special when wearing it.

**Parisian Party:** Paris is known for being the "center of the universe" when it comes to the Art Deco movement in design and style. What ways can vintage jewelry be incorporated into a French wedding look, in particular, if a couple wants to play up Paris during les années folles?

**Heidi Ellis:** Many a bride has found her treasure in Au Grenier de Lucie. As jewelry is timeless, any of the pieces can be incorporated into a wedding look. Some girls love the pieces from the 30s and 40s, whereas others opt for contemporary designs that use vintage components. The key to success is finding that piece that adds the finishing touch. Some of the key jewelry designers from the Art Deco era were Chanel, Miriam Haskell and Elsa Schiaparelli. All three designers

were committed to fashion and were rivals in their day. The 20s and 30s are so nostalgic and it is easy to understand why weddings depicting this era are so popular today. Finding pieces by these three designers from this era are rare. However, we do come across them from time to time, and they find their way into many ladies' treasure-troves.

**Parisian Party:** Vintage designer jewelry pieces can often carry a pretty big price tag. You also sell certain lines in your shop that are new pieces made from repurposed, high-end costume jewelry. This can sometimes offer an alternative for brides on a budget. Can you tell me a bit about some of these newer designers, and what was it about them that attracted you to carry them in your shop alongside the classics?

**Heidi Ellis:** Bijoux Heart is a favorite of ours. They create the most beautiful, unique modern pieces made of vintage stones and modern crystals. Their designs and colors are exquisite, and the craftsmanship is truly remarkable, as Tracy Graham and her partner Robbie are so committed and passionate about their work. We're delighted to be the only boutique in France offering their line of jewelry. We also like to encourage young Parisian designers such as Kormilitz, who uses vintage components in her designs as well. It was wonderful to see her excitement when we agreed to become her first point of sale in Paris. We feel it's so important to support new, aspiring, young designers.

For us, it's essential to house a range of designs to cater for all tastes. We have one rule: If it is beautiful, then we have a place for it in our boutique!

Au Grenier de Lucie
Marché Vernaison, Allée 1 stand 25,
99, rue de Rosiers, Saint-Ouen
www.augrenierdelucie.com

Bijoux Heart
www.bijoux-heart.com

Kormelitz
http://kormelitz.com

# French Wedding Menu Demystified: L'Apéritif

Wikipedia describes an *apéritif* (Fr.) as "an alcoholic drink usually enjoyed as an appetizer before a large meal. It is often served with something small to eat, like olives or crackers." If you're planning a wedding or event in France, and you're looking at catering menus, you'll notice that there are several drink standards that are almost always on offer during an apéritif (or *apéro,* as it's casually known in France), with some modifications being made depending on the region of France that you're in. I've taken the liberty to sample quite a few of these over the years and now give you my rather girlie definition of the following:

**Kir:** A sweet little cocktail made with crème de cassis (blackcurrant liqueur) and topped with white wine. Kir can also be ordered in peach, strawberry or blackberry. I think they're delicious and very girlie (even though French men drink them all the time, but they also wear their sweaters tied around their shoulders even though it's not 1986 nor are they on the tennis court. AND they proudly walk those itty-bitty Paris Hilton-type dogs in public. Just saying.) A Kir Royale takes it up a notch by being made with sparkling wine or Champagne instead of wine.

**Pastis:** This is strong, cloudy-yellow, licorice-flavored alcohol that's popular in the South of France. When you order a Pastis, you get served a tall, thin glass with about two inches of alcohol with an iced-tea spoon and a small pitcher of water on the side. You pour the water into the Pastis to dilute it to your taste. I remember my first sip of pastis tasting a tad bit better than Everclear, but around four sips in, it's really not so bad!

**Ricard:** Honestly, I don't know the difference between this and Pastis. I think Ricard may be cloudy white as opposed to Pastis being yellow, but perhaps someone can send me a note to enlighten me.

**Martini (rouge or blanc):** This isn't a *martini* martini (of the "shaken not stirred" variety) but straight vermouth poured over the rocks. This is my father-in-law's preferred apéro, and it really isn't so bad. Order this one to impress your visiting friends and relatives with your Frenchiness (every tourist knows about the kir thing by now!).

**Muscat:** This yummy sweet white wine is served a bit cold (a very refreshing alternative here in this "Land O' No Ice").

**Port:** Port is the same as in the United States, but in France, people drink it before instead of after dinner.

In addition to the alcoholic beverages, an apéritif menu will also include *boissons non alcoolisées* (non-alcoholic beverages), called "softs" in French. This includes orange juice, Coke/Diet Coke, water (both fizzy and not), etc.

An apéritif menu will also often offer *amuse bouches* (literally, "mouth amuses" [bouche = mouth; amuser = to amuse, to please]). There usually isn't much of an explanation of the amuse bouches on the menu because it depends on what you select as your starter and/or main course. The price of the amuse bouches is typically included in the price of the apéro, and there isn't a selection. Everyone gets the same thing. It could be as simple as olives or something a bit more elaborate like mozzarella-stuffed tomatoes or melon wrapped with a *jambon cru* (dry-cured ham).

One thing that can be confusing about French wedding menus is knowing the difference between a *"vin d'honneur,"* a cocktail, and an apéritif. The three terms seem to be used interchangeably in France, but there can be subtle differences. Directly following a typical French wedding ceremony, you will be invited to a vin d'honneur, usually in or nearby the ceremony venue. There you'll be served Champagne to drink, but more than likely there will also be apéritif standards on hand (see page 155). At the vin d'honneur, you'll have a chance to snack on small, salty amuse bouches (think mini quiche or mini blinis), and simple, sweet hors d'oeuvres. Later on at the reception venue, there is often an apéritif or cocktail before dinner, more standard cocktail drinks than Champagne this time, lighter on the amuse bouches and more substantial hors d'oeuvres (both sweet and salty). After guests are seated, they will then be served their starter, and then dinner, dessert and dancing.

You don't need much to bring the French apéro to your Parisian-themed wedding or party, but here's a simple French amuse bouche recipe to get you started (facing page), from www.easy-french-food.com. *Tchin-tchin!*

## DIY CHIC PARISIAN DESSERT

How about this for a fabulous Parisian dessert . . . or is it a cocktail? For the past eighty years, Paris restaurant La Maison Prunier in the 16th arrondissement has been world renowned for its exquisite selection of caviar. Now it has taken things up a notch by combining lime sorbet, Malossol caviar and Champagne Nicolas Feuillate Cuvée Palmes d'Or Vintage 1998 to create a wickedly sublime concoction. Extraordinarily chic yet simple to re-create *chez toi* (at home), this recipe is sure to add a Parisian touch to your next soirée, whether you serve it as a cocktail or dessert.

LA MAISON PRUNIER
15, Victor Hugo
75016 Paris, France
www.prunier.com

ESPACE NICOLAS FEUILLATE
254, rue du Faubourg Saint-Honoré
75008 Paris, France
www.nicolas-feuillatte.com

GLACIER BERTILLION
29-31, rue Saint-Louis en l'Ile
75004 Paris, France
www.berthillon.fr

# ROULADE JAMBON CHEVRE

### INGREDIENTS

2 tablespoons Parmesan cheese

8 ounces soft goat cheese
  (not the kind with a rind)

2 tablespoons chopped fresh herbs
  (try mint, parsley, chives, dill or
  your favorites)

2 tablespoons olive oil

Salt and pepper

8 ounces sliced cooked ham
  (luncheon meat style)

Curry powder (optional)

### DIRECTIONS

In a food processor, blend the Parmesan
cheese, goat cheese, herbs and olive oil
together until smooth. Season with salt and
pepper. Lay the ham slices flat and spread
evenly with the cheese mixture. Roll up the
ham and slice into bite-sized servings. For
an extra touch of color and taste, dip the
end of the roll in curry powder.

# Tête à Tête with Wedding Stationery Designers Paper + Cup

I've always found it a little surprising that letterpress stationery is so hard to come by in Paris. While you can find options for good-quality customizable wedding invitations in any number of papeteries around Paris, the hip and stylish contemporary letterpress suites that are de rigueur on today's American bridal and social scene just haven't been on the radar in France.

Enter Paper + Cup, a New York–based stationery and graphic design company headed by husband-and-wife team Minhee and Thomas Cho. Paper + Cup specializes in letterpress wedding invitations, note cards, journals and gift tags, with products sold through their design studio, online shop and in more than 250 stores across the United States. When their designer, Sarah, decided to move back to her native Paris, they jumped at the opportunity to go global and had her bring the innovative, modern, vintage-infused designs of Paper + Cup with her. Since 2011, destination and European wedding clients have been able to get Paper + Cup's "fresh invitations and stylish paper designs" on both sides of the Atlantic through Sarah's design studio, Mister M. I met up with Sarah in her studio in the funky 9th arrondissement to talk about French wedding etiquette and paper trends for the modern Parisian bride.

**Parisian Party**: What are the differences between modern Parisian wedding stationery design and modern New York wedding stationery?

Paper + Cup's "stylish paper designs" can be found on both sides of the *Atlantic.* They create classic designs with a *twist* for Parisian clients as well as nontraditional, *out—of—the—box* designs for New Yorkers.

**Paper + Cup**: Until recently, Parisian wedding stationery was very classical, with almost no design, but just simple calligraphy on a quality paper. Thanks to the Internet and U.S. wedding blogs especially, Parisians have become aware that they could do something more "design" for their wedding stationery. Parisians tend to go for more classic designs with a twist whereas New Yorkers are more open to trying something totally nontraditional and out of the box.

**Parisian Party**: Being so classic and traditional, I'd imagine there would be a certain level of protocol surrounding social stationery in France. What are some of the "dos and don'ts" of French wedding invitations?

**Paper + Cup**: I think that the French definitely have more formal guidelines when it comes to wording wedding invitations. For example, the parents of both the bride and groom are almost always mentioned. And listing "no children" or a specific dress code would be considered a very big faux pas.

**Parisian Party**: What are the current trends that you see coming out of Paris as far as wedding stationery?

**Paper + Cup**: Pocket folders are really popular with our French wedding clients, which makes sense because they have so many different components to include (individual cards for the civil and/or church ceremonies, plus the various cocktail receptions and parts of the dinner that make up the typical French wedding day). French couples also have a great eye for color combinations, particularly in pastels and soft shades. Right now our French brides are really into subtle vintage touches like luggage tags for place cards or customized wooden stamps for their return address, for example.

**Parisian Party**: What are some ways that an American bride planning a wedding in the States can add a Parisian touch to her wedding stationery suite?

**Paper + Cup**: It's all in the details, Parisians are all about details. Some common themes for French-style weddings can be Marie Antoinette or the Chateau de Versailles. But to avoid looking clichéd, brides can take a few subtle hints and incorporate them throughout their wedding stationery. Perhaps it's just a color scheme, a pastel *poudré* (powder), for example, a pretty pattern or iconic symbol. The key is to not go overboard.

Find daily design inspirations from both Paris and New York on papercupsketchbook.com, the blog of Paper + Cup Designs.

PAPER + CUP
www.papercupdesigns.com

MISTER M STUDIO
www.mistermstudio.com

# Paris Wedding Hairstyles: The Chignon

As with wine, cheese, fashion and Johnny Halliday, the French take their chignons very seriously. Before moving to France, I had assumed that a chignon was a fancy word for "bun"—when hair is pulled back into a band and then pinned under to make, well, a bun. It wasn't until I started phoning hair salons in Paris for wedding clients did I realize how naive I had been. The moment that I would tell the salon receptionist that my client needed a chignon, her tone would immediately change: "Non! Zayre ees nobody who can do chignon 'eere." Or, "C'est pas possible, Pierre is zee only one who can do chignon and Thursday ees his day off!" That was my first clue that a chignon *à la française* is a whole other ballgame.

*Bombée, tressé, néo-romantique, décoiffé* or *banane*—the names of styles of the French chignon are as elaborate as the many variations of the style itself. Like the bride who sports it, a classic *chignon mariage* can be austere, demure or unbridled. It can be slicked back, poofed up, or swept over with meters of ringlets tumbling down the bride's back. Some French hairstylists devote their entire professional lives to chignon, while others, having been shamed early on in beauty school, outright refuse to approach them. This is actually quite a noble thing, considering that a bad chignon is typically very, *very* bad.

When you're making an appointment for a chignon at a salon in Paris, especially for a wedding or other special occasion, try to make an appointment for a trial (called an *essai* in French) sometime before the actual event. Go to the trial armed with photos of the style you want, any combs, clips or other accessories that you plan to wear and photos of your wedding dress or gown. This being Paris, be prepared for the stylist to gasp in horror at your photos, and to insist that under no circumstance will he ever give you the style that you want. It's okay, it's all part of *le jeu* (the game). Let him give you the style that he thinks is best, ogle and fawn all over it, all the while flaming his ego with words like *"maître"* (master) and *"génie"* (genius). Then slowly ease it into the style you want. For example: "Oh, Pierre, it is absolutely *magnifique* (magnificent)! My future sister-in-law was right! You ARE a genius. You have given me a chignon that is sexy and sophisticated, with just the right amount of virginity to make those other women seethe with jealousy. Oh, but I must confess—I have always been embarrassed by the homeliness of the nape of my neck. Do you think it would be possible to drop the chignon down just a bit, to spare me the embarrassment on my wedding day?"

Many salons in Paris will offer a *forfait mariage*, which is a package deal that could include a hair and makeup trial, plus hair/makeup and a simple manicure on the day of. The prices of forfait mariage are varied. For some reason, salons in Paris are usually very suspicious about quoting a forfait price over the phone. They often try to insist that you come in to see them to get a price. If you let them know that you're phoning from overseas and are unable to come in, they will give you a price seemingly off the top of their heads, but you can assume that the true price will be within fifty euros or so of the one quoted. The best bet, of course, is if you have a printed advertisement or if you can get a quote sent to you by email.

If you're thinking about trying out an authentic French chignon while in Paris, take a look at a few of these salons. I'm sure that any one of them will make you look magnifique.

BAR À CHIGNONS
Christophe-Nicolas Biot
52, rue Saint André des Arts
75006 Paris, France
www.christophenicolasbiot.com/

CARITA INTERNATIONAL
11, rue du Faubourg Saint-Honoré
75008 Paris, France
www.carita.com

JEAN MARC JOUBERT
255, rue Saint-Honoré
75001 Paris, France
www.jeanmarcjoubert.com

# French Wedding Flower Traditions

There's an old French wedding tradition, still practiced in some parts of France I hear, where the groom chooses and buys the bride's bouquet, then presents it to her when he picks her up on the way to the wedding ceremony. Can you imagine? I even found an article that gave these nuggets of advice to the hapless groom-to-be:

---

### OLD-FASHIONED ADVICE FOR THE FRENCH GROOM

"As the groom often can not see the dress before the wedding, the bride should give him some pointers so that the ensemble will be harmonious.

The choice of bouquet is as follows:

⚜ If the dress is long, the choice should be a vast bouquet, trailing, round or discreet. If the dress is short, the bouquet should be round or rather discreet so as not to mask the dress.

⚜ You also need to know that the more elaborate and large a bouquet is, the heavier it is, and therefore it may embarrass the bride.

⚜ Colored flowers are great, but the dominant color of a bridal bouquet is usually white even if different colored wedding gowns are growing increasingly popular these days."

---

And so, armed with these little tidbits, the French groom is sent on his way.

Luckily, this tradition does seem to have fallen by the wayside. With multiple picture-postcard flower shops dotting nearly every neighborhood, modern Parisian brides have no problem choosing and making their own decisions about the flowers for their wedding.

One of the cutest Parisian florists is Lieu-Dit Atelier Floral. A fixture in historical Montparnasse since the 1980s, Lieu-Dit is best known for its natural and harmonious approach to floral design. Owners Mina and Alain and I talked about the Paris bride's approach to choosing flowers for her wedding.

**Lieu-Dit:** Parisian brides typically choose white or very pale pastel colors for their wedding flowers, with roses, peonies, orchids and callas being the most requested. For a soft, romantic look, we'll mix in sweet peas, ranunculus, anemones and, depending on the season, muguet (lily of the valley) for May, or Christmas roses for a winter bride. While classic round bouquets will always be popular, we also have many requests for cascading bouquets as well. The cascade bouquet is very popular for French brides. For a clean, timeless look, many Parisian brides will carry modern bouquets of long, white callas as well.

For the church, French couples tend to be rather conservative. We'll do different variations of white—vanilla, blanc cassé or a creamy yellow for the church floral arrangements. For the wedding reception, French brides will be more adventurous and add bursts of color to their dinner décor.

"It's this slight emphasis on *elegance* that makes a *French—inspired* wedding so special."

**Parisian Party:** What are some of the current trends in Parisian wedding flower design?

**Lieu-Dit:** I find that French brides don't really follow trends when it comes to their wedding flowers. Although with more French brides reading the American wedding blogs, we are starting to receive certain "typically American" requests, like tall table centers, for instance. French brides tend to be more discrete in their bouquets and centerpieces. The bridal bouquet is smaller for French brides than American ones, for instance. In France, we usually make the bridal bouquet just a little bit smaller than the bride's face. It's this slight emphasis on elegance that makes a French-inspired wedding so special and these sorts of fine details can be brought to French-inspired weddings anywhere.

In addition to providing floral décor to many designer boutiques around town (Armani, Cerruti and Versace, to name a few) Lieu-Dit also hosts floral arts classes for an international clientele, where they teach eager students the subtle nuances of French floral arts.

LIEU-DIT ARTS FLORAL
21, avenue du Maine
75015 Paris, France
www.lieu-dit-paris.fr

## FRENCH WEDDING ACCESSORY: CUSTOM FANS

If you're looking for ways to personalize a 1920s Paris- or Art Deco–themed wedding, why not consider forgoing the traditional flower bouquet and carry a beautiful handmade fan from France instead? Originally a clothing designer, Olivia Oberlin fell in love with fans in the mid-90s, and went on to study for two years with a master fan-maker under the patronage of the French Ministry of Culture. Now she and her assistants create bespoke fans for customers all over the world. Olivia Oberlin Eventails uses antique as well as contemporary materials, and works carefully to make every fan exactly to their clients' wishes. Her collections have names like "Temptation" and "Lumière" and are painstakingly constructed out of materials like ostrich feathers, Calais lace and silk shantung. Not only a dramatic statement coming down the aisle, but a custom fan can add that extra a bit of French flair during your reception or on the dance floor at the after-party. They could also be offered as a beautiful bridesmaids gift or simply as a lovely souvenir of Paris for special guests.

OLIVIA OBERLIN EVENTAILS
www.olivia-oberlin.com

# BLAIR & JUDSON

From the morning preparations in a stunning, turn-of-the-century private apartment by the Seine, through to the romantic slow dance at the top of Trocadero in all of it's Art Deco glory, Judson and Blair's sophisticated, subtly vintage wedding celebration was a true Moveable Feast.

WEDDING DESIGN AND COORDINATION
Kim Petyt
Parisian Events
www.parisianevents.com

PHOTOGRAPHY
Heidi Geldhauser
www.ourlaboroflove.com

FLORIST
Atelier Lieu-Dit
www.lieu-dit-paris.fr

DRESS
Casablanca Couture
www.casablancabridal.com

PARIS DANCE INSTRUCTOR
Marc Reed
www.marcreed.net

# Credits &
# Additional Resources

## PHOTOGRAPHERS

DAVID BACHER
www.photobacher.com
55-57, 127,164 (left)

HEIDI GELDHAUSER
www.ourlaboroflove.com
19, 26,29,75,166-173

CORBIN GURKIN
www.corbingurkin.com
119,120

IAN HOLMES
www.ianholmes.net
1,6,8,15,27,31, 42-45, 66-72,78,
86-89,94,110-113, 129 (top &
bottom),131,134-143, 144-147,
154-157, 160, 163, 164 (right)

MILOS & NATASA HORVAT
www.miloshorvat.com
10,12,13, 32-41, 100-109,124, back
cover

ARMAN MOLAVI
www.armanimage.com
20,21,30,49,51,79-85,161

CLÉLIA NAUD
www.hypiness.blogspot.fr
17

CATHERINE OHARA PHOTOGRAPHY
www.catherineohara.com
99

ONE AND ONLY PARIS PHOTOGRAPHY
www.oneandonlyparisphotography.
com
14, 16 (for www.monplusbeaujour.
com), 23, 24 (top), 46-47, 58-65,
128

ROBERT & KATHLEEN TREMSKE
www.robertandkathleen.com
cover photo, 117, 118

ZHOU XIAONAN - PHOTO ZHOU
www.photozhou.com
148-151

Page 53: image courtesy of Laduree
Page 54: image © elen_studio, used
    under license from Shutterstock.
    com
Page 74: image courtesy of Graine
    de Coton
Page 76: Image courtesy Fouquet's
    Barrière
Pages 50—53, 90 (top), 91: images
    courtesy of Loanna Haseltine
Pages 90 (bottom), 93: images ©
    Steven Lyon, courtesy of Loanna
    Haseltine

Page 114: image courtesy of Rein-
    aldo Alvarez
Psge 115: image courtesy of Rachel
    Freed
Page 121: photo courtesy of Sugar-
    plum Cake Shop
Pages 123 and 125 (upper and lower):
    images courtesy of Yachts de Paris
Pages 132—33: images courtesy of
    Melissa Regan de Vogele, Vouelle
Pages 158—59: images courtesy of
    Paper + Cup Design
Page 165: Images courtesy of Ober-
    lin Evantails

## WEDDING STATIONERY

CT DESIGNS & CALLIGRAPHY
www.ct-designs.com

MISTER M STUDIO
www.mistermstudio.com

PAPER + CUP DESIGNS
www.papercupdesign.com

## VENUES

LADURÉE
75, Champs-Elysées
75008 Paris, France
www.laduree.fr

MACEO RESTAURANT
15, rue des Petits Champs
75001 Paris
www.maceorestaurant.com

MAISON POLYTECHNICIENS
12, rue de Poitiers
75007 Paris
www.maisondesx.com

RESTAURANT DE BAGATELLE
42, Route de Sèvres à Neuilly
75016 Paris, France

SALON DES MIROIRS
13, Passage Jouffroy
75009 Paris, France
www.salon-miroirs.com

YACHTS DE PARIS
Port Henri IV
75004 Paris, France
www.entreprises.yachtsdeparis.fr

## GOWNS & ATTIRE

REINALDO ALVAREZ
9, rue Jarente
75004 Paris, France
www.reinaldo-alvarez.com

AU GRENIER DE LUCIE
Marché Vernaison, allée 1 stand 25
99, rue de rosiers, saint-ouen
www.augrenierdelucie.com

HASELTINE
67, rue Reaumur
75002 Paris, France
www.haseltine-paris.com

FANNY LIAUTARD
13, rue Saint-Florentin
75008 Paris, France
www.fannyliautard.com

ANA QUASOAR
7, rue Banque
75002, Paris France
www.anaquasoar.com

VOUELLE
167, boulevard Haussemann
75008 Paris, France
www.vouelle.com

## MISCELLANEOUS PARIS WEDDING RESOURCES

CHAUFFEUR
American Driver in Paris
Christian Mayer
www.americandriverinparis.com

HAIR & MAKEUP
By James
www.jmsbyjames.com

TAILOR-MADE WEDDING
ILLUSTRATIONS & ACCESSORIES
Astrid Mueller
www.astridmuellerexclusive.com

WEDDING & PARTY RENTALS
Aktuel
www.aktuel.fr

# About the Author

After experiencing firsthand the complexities of planning her own wedding in France from a distance in 2000, Kimberley Petyt decided to create Parisian Events, a wedding and event-planning agency catering to English-speakers in Paris. With more than ten years of experience planning corporate and social events in both the United States and France, Petyt has become a true Paris insider. She writes the popular blog Parisian Party: Tales of an American Wedding Planner in Paris (parisianevents.com/parisianparty/), which was voted 2010 Best International Wedding Blog by AOL's wedding website, Aisledash.com.

Petyt is known to be a preeminent resource for planning a wedding or special event in Paris. Since founding Parisian Events in 2005, both Petyt and the business have received international attention, including appearances on international television, and references in print publications including *Real Simple Weddings, Los Angeles Times, Essence Magazine, Eco-Beautiful Weddings, Long Island Bride & Groom, Cosmopolitan China,* and *France Magazine.* Most recently, she was featured in the *New York Times T Magazine* "Summer 2011 Travel" issue, highlighting her skills as a cultural liaison for brides seeking to marry in Paris.